JOURNEY
to the
LONELY CHRIST

* * *

Milestones In The Life
of
Catherine de Hueck Doherty

* * *

Aug. 15, 1896 - Born in a Pullman car near Nijni-Novgorod (present day Gorki) in Russia, the second of 7 children: Natasha, who died as a young child, three brothers who died in miscarriages, and two young brothers — Serge, who was born in Egypt, and Andrew, who was born when the family returned to Russia.

1902 - Accompanies family to Alexandria, Egypt where she receives her first formal education. Brother Serge is born.

Jan. 25, 1915 - Marries Baron Boris de Hueck in St. Petersburg.

1917 - Fled to England during the Russian revolution. Nearly starved.

1918 - Liberated by White Russian soldiers. Went to Murmansk where she and her husband were warmly received by the British.

1919 - Went to Scotland, then to England.

1921 - Arrived in Toronto, Canada. In July, her son, George, is born.

1930 - Founded Friendship House on Portland street.

1933 - Began Newspaper, *The Social Forum.*

1934 - Founded house in Ottawa.

1935 - Founded house in Hamilton.

1936 - Forced to close house in Toronto. Boris finds work in Montreal; goes his separate way. Catherine meets and becomes friends with Dorothy Day of the *Catholic Worker* Movement.

1937 - Sent to Europe by Archbishop McGuigan (Toronto) to investigate Catholic Action groups in Portugal, Spain and France. Also visits Belgium, Poland and Czechoslovakia.

1938 - Invited by Cardinal Patrick Hayes of New York to open house in Harlem, at 135th and Lennox.

1939 - Lectured on the Chatauqua circuit throughout the U.S.

1940 - Receives a Church annulment of her first marriage. Begins Newspaper, *Friendship House News*. Son, Geroge, in military service.

1941 - Becomes friends with Thomas Merton who is much influenced by her lifestyle.

1942 - Founds Friendship House in Chicago.

June 25, 1943 - Married Eddie Doherty, both of whose former marriages had ended with the death of his wife.

1946 - *Friendship House* (out of print)
- Rejected by the Friendship House Staff in Chicago.

1947 - *Dear Bishop* (out of print)
- Left the U.S. for Canada where, on May 17, 1947, she founded the Madonna House Settlement in Combermere, Ontario. Her son, George, graduates from Queens University.

Jan., 1948 - Eddie Doherty suffers first heart attack.

1950 - *Dear Seminarian* (out of print)

1952 - *Where Love Is, God Is* (out of print)

1956 - Her first husband, Boris, the Baron de Hueck, dies.

1975 - *Poustinia* (Ave Maria Press)
- Her second husband, Eddie Doherty, dies.

1976 - *The Gospel Without Compromise* (Ave Maria Press)

1977 - *Sobornost* (Ave Maria Press)
- *Not Without Parables* (Ave Maria Press)

1978 - *Strannik* (Ave Maria Press)
- *The People of the Towel and the Water* (Dimension Books)

1979 - *Unknown Mysteries of Our Lady* (Dimension Books)
- *Dear Father* (Alba House)
- *I Live on an Island* (Ave Maria Press)
- *Fragments of My Life* (Ave Maria Press)

1981 - *Doubts, Loneliness, Rejection* (Alba House)
- University of St. Michael's College, Toronto, awards her an honorary Doctors Degree in Sacred Letters.
- Became seriously ill in August and remained such off and on till her death in 1985.

1982 - *Molchanie: The Silence of God* (Crossroad)

1983 - *Urodovoi: Fools for God* (Crossroad)

1984 - *Journey Inward* (Alba House)

Dec. 14, 1985 - Passed to her eternal reward. She leaves behind her, besides her countless writings, some twenty Madonna House communities: 10 in Canada, 7 in the United States, 1 in France, 1 in Barbados and 1 in England.

JOURNEY
to the
LONELY CHRIST

* * *

The Little Mandate
of
Catherine de Hueck Doherty

by

Robert Wild

ALBA·HOUSE   NEW·YORK

SOCIETY OF ST. PAUL, 2187 VICTORY BLVD., STATEN ISLAND, NEW YORK 10314

Library of Congress Cataloging in Publication Data

Wild, Robert A., 1936 -
  Journey to the lonely Christ

  Bibliography: p.
  1. Doherty, Catherine de Hueck, 1900 -
2. Catholics — Biography.   3. Spirituality — Catholic
Church — History of doctrines — 20th century.   4. Catholic
Church — Doctrines — History — 20th century.   I. Title.

BX4705.D64W55   1987   248.4'82   86-17388
ISBN 0-8189-0509-3

Designed, printed and bound in the United States of
America by the Fathers and Brothers of the
Society of St. Paul, 2187 Victory Boulevard,
Staten Island, New York 10314, as part of their
communications apostolate.

---

2 3 4 5 6 7 8 9 (Current Printing: first digit)

Table Of Contents

* * *

Introduction

* * *

Catherine de Hueck Doherty died December 14, 1985, 5:30 A.M., the feast of St. John of the Cross, in her cabin in Combermere, Ontario, Canada. A few minutes after her death her bed was surrounded by her spiritual children of Madonna House. Her life and teaching influenced millions of people. It is safe to say that she was one of the great women of our century, perhaps of all time. History will decide.

Who was she? She would have answered, "I am a woman in love with God and with the poor." This tells all. But people in love with God assume many forms. In this introduction to a study of her spirituality I would like to develop briefly the biblical figure of the prophet, and say that Catherine Doherty was a prophet, a prophet seized and slain by certain words of God, overpowered by them, even (in the strong words of Jeremiah) "seduced" by them. Her life and teaching was the living expression of these words.

What words? She often told us. She called them her "Little Mandate," which is the subject of the present book. "Little," because she saw herself as of no account or consequence; "Mandate," because she really experienced them as coming from God, as being mandated by him. She had an extraordinary sense of having been called to some special mission by God himself. We cannot speak of her spirituality without reference to these words. I quote them here in full:

> Arise — go? Sell all you possess . . . give it directly, personally to the poor. Take up My cross (their cross) and follow Me — going to the poor — being poor — being one with them — one with Me.
>
> Little — be always little . . . simple — poor — childlike.
>
> Preach the Gospel WITH YOUR LIFE — WITHOUT COMPROMISE — listen to the Spirit — He will lead you.
>
> Do little things exceedingly well for love of Me.
>
> Love — love — love, never counting the cost.
>
> Go into the marketplace and stay with Me . . . pray . . . fast . . . pray always . . . fast.
>
> Be hidden — be a light to your neighbor's feet. Go without fears into the depth of men's hearts . . . I shall be with you.
>
> Pray always. I WILL BE YOUR REST.

Now a prophet is a totally contemporary person, that is, he or she sees the present with the eyes of God. The words they have received can never be totally understood or explained in terms of their life experiences; still, their life experiences form the prism through which the words they have received mature, are understood by them, and are expressed. Therefore, we must look briefly at her life (especially if the present reader is unfamiliar with it). Her life spanned almost the whole of the 20th century (1896-1985), and she was involved in its dramas as very few people have been.

Born in Nijni-Novgorod (now Gorki), she experienced the relative luxury and wholeness of life in pre-revolutionary Russia. She was a nurse in the First World War and was decorated for bravery. She stood in the crowd in front of the Smolensky Institute as Lenin, in 1917, presented his dark plan for the new earthly paradise. She experienced the confiscation of all her possessions and the loss of many of her relatives. She had to flee the country, and thus knew the condition of a refugee — what it was to be driven from one's beloved country.

She knew what it was to be without a country, and then to be taken in by a friendly nation (Canada). She experienced the bottom of the social ladder, and then, through her lecturing, wealth in the land of opportunity. She knew marriage, the birth and raising of a child, and the tragic dissolution of a marriage. Believing in the power of love, she dared to fall in love again, and marry again.

She knew how to sway audiences in her public addresses on Russia and on social conditions in North America. She knew how to chit-chat with the poor as she handed out clothes and food in the slums of the New World. She knew the terror of fighting racial prejudice in both the Church and society. She was the foundress of Friendship Houses across America, and, before her death, missions of Madonna House across the world.

She was friends with Cardinal Cushing in Boston, Jacques Maritain in France, and Julia Mayhew, her neighbor across the street in Combermere.

Through these and countless other experiences the words of the Little Mandate grew and deepened in her heart, and expressed themselves ever more concretely in her life and teaching. She has left an immense body of teaching, most of which has not yet been published. When it is published, what will be its significance?

It will be seen as a totally contemporary gospel spirituality which goes to the essence of our ancient faith while avoiding the aberrations of the modern world. We will not be able to say that she was "unaware" of this or that facet of our contemporary situation. As a true prophet, *she was aware*.

Orthodox and Roman; Russian and North American; Old World and New World; pre-modern and post-modern; pre-Vatican II and post-Vatican II; lone apostle and foundress of a community; criss-crossing the world, speaking, ministering to the poor, challenging people to love the God-Man whose love has been rejected — of all people of our times, Catherine Doherty was aware, totally present in our world.

The fundamental question her life and teaching will pose is this: Can we accept her total vision, or will we pick and choose what we want? Like her, can we be both in the poustina and in the marketplace? Can we love the Church as the Spouse of Christ, and weep over its failings? Can we love the suffering Christ in everyone, rich and poor alike? Can we live and preach the whole Gospel without watering it down to what people like to hear? Can we use the full capacity of our minds and hearts but always subjecting them to the light of faith? Can we face realistically the tragedies of the world — which are immense at this time — without losing the joy of the risen Christ?

At a time in history when, to many people, "Russia" means the "evil empire," God sent us a woman from Holy Russia who, as well as anyone in our time, taught and incarnated the "empire of love." If she truly was a prophet sent from God, will we have the courage to follow her?

One evening towards the end of 1982, I was visiting Catherine in her cabin. We were talking about Madonna House and her publications. I told her that I had envisioned — in ten years or so — putting together into a book my course on the Little Mandate. (I had been teaching this course for the past few years to those aspiring to join our religious family.) She said: "Now's the time."

Presenting the Gospel vision of this great woman is a formidable task because of the richness and extensiveness of her writings. But after that conversation with her, and after consultation here with those responsible, it seemed the Lord's will to try and articulate, in some limited way, her spirituality. First, what am I attempting? Secondly, what are the limitations or boundaries of this presentation?

In several volumes, of which this is the first, I am attempting a simple, straight-forward presentation of the spirituality of the Little Mandate, the Lord's words to her which I have quoted above.

Catherine considers these words to be the heart and essence of her own personal vocation. Her whole teaching can be considered as a further elaboration of these words.

Already people are beginning to write dissertations and theses on her spirituality. The material available for these studies is very limited. I consider the Staff Letters (SL) she has written to her spiritual family over the years as the most important part of her teaching, and none of these has yet been published. I thought it would be helpful to present, from Madonna House itself, and using many of our primary sources, a vision of the heart of her spirituality which might then serve as some kind of guideline for people's study and reflection.

I will try mostly to present her doctrine using *her own words* and not mine. Some commentary will be unavoidable; the selection of material is already a kind of commentary. But my real intention is to allow you to listen to Catherine herself, to hear the music of her new song flowing from her own great mind and heart. I will be making some comments about the origins of her spirituality, but this is not a major consideration; I will be saying a few things about the biblical roots of her doctrine, but neither is this a primary focus. It's *her own words* I'd like you to hear.

A further clarification is necessary: Catherine's teaching is very extensive. I do not intend to touch on every aspect of it. There is this core which she calls the Little Mandate. It is the deep fountain out of which her whole spirituality flows. I think I have personally arrived at the point where I see how all the major themes of this Mandate fit together. This is the vision I wish to present.

I teach another course here at Madonna House which concerns our Constitution or Way of Life. This includes both spirituality and its practical application to our daily life. In the present book you will not find much practical application. I'm interested in the spiritual fountain out of which all the applications flow.

There are certain dangers in doing it this way. One aspect of her genius is precisely not having doctrine separate from application to daily life.

She often says that all real spirituality must be incarnate. So this book must be seen as part of a larger presentation, which will grow and expand as more of her works are published. I offer here only a modest beginning, nothing more. I have read almost all of her writings. This should give the reader confidence that the present work flows from familiarity with these primary sources.

A few years ago the Catholic University of America put out a series called *The Catholic Tradition*. The stated purpose of the series was to "select from the Catholic Tradition the 200 greatest writers of all time." In Volume 14, the second of two volumes on spirituality, Catherine is listed along with Francis de Sales, Teresa of Avila, Cardinal Newman and others. This means that already Catherine is considered, at least by some, as one of the greatest teachers of the Gospel of all time. The excerpts in Volume 14 are from *Poustinia*, which is truly a great book — but the best is yet to come!

It is a great privilege to help propagate her vision. It can truthfully be said that already her writings are giving life to millions of people. I believe this is only the beginning.

History will decide. I really think, though, that her influence will be greater than anyone now realizes or appreciates.

This book is a small tribute to a great woman. I wish with all my heart it were better than it is.

Compiling it is an act of personal love for her as well as a way of saying thank you to the Lord. May it serve, in some modest way, to help others understand a vision of life which is truly one of the most remarkable ever inspired by the Holy Spirit.

When I told Catherine the title I had selected, she said, "That's a wonderful title. That's what I have been trying to do from the beginning" (that is, journey to the lonely Christ).

The Little Mandate
of
Catherine de Hueck Doherty

CHAPTER ONE

Foundations

* * *

The Nature Of The Mandate

One of the most fundamental documents we have from Catherine is a tape she made on April 27, 1968, which is entitled simply, "Little Mandate" (LM). We often refer to it as the tape on "How the Little Mandate Came To Be." The first few paragraphs of this tape give an important insight into the nature of the Mandate:

It is a spring day, gray, but with a little bit of sunshine. I am trying to gather my thoughts to make a tape on the background of the Little Mandate. I said to myself, I'd better give a background to the Mandate because, in its present form, it may seem that one blessed day some angel, or God, or our Blessed Mother, in some miraculous way dictated this thing to me and it all came out in one piece, like a Hail Mary. Well, it is far from being the case. And it is because it is so far from being the case that I thought I'd better give that background.

Now, I confess, it is not an easy thing to do. It means turning my spiritual footsteps backwards into the past. I can't say it's an unpainful past; I would be a liar. All

through my life I have had a modicum of peace, God's
peace, and it grew with the years. Added to that, I had the
strange joy of God which very quietly lay in the cradle of
pain.

How big the joy, how big the peace, only God knows.
But my mother's words (spoken) at birth — "You are born
under the shadow of the Cross" — have come to pass.
Probably she meant giving birth to me in a pullman car,
which must have been a great cross to her. But that is what
she told me when I was older, and I remember that now.
Slowly, personally, day by day, hour by hour, minute by
minute as I grew older, the meaning of those words grow
deeper and deeper and deeper.   (HMCB)

There is an idea in these paragraphs which is a key to an
understanding of the nature of the Little Mandate: The
words of the Mandate did not drop *ready-made* from heaven,
but grew in her mind and heart over the years.

When God wishes to accomplish something in the
world, he speaks to somebody, puts words of life into his or
her heart, which continue to grow and become clearer. I
think each of us has a Little Mandate, words that came to us
in prayer, or through experience, or through reading,
which sort of form the foundation of our lives. These are the
words we revert to in times of decisions; these are the words
which give our lives meaning and direction at the deepest
level.

A full understanding of the Little Mandate of
Catherine would entail a full understanding of her life, and
especially the circumstances which fostered these particular
words. As I mentioned, brief indications will be given to
those events in this book, though I will not go into her life
very much. The more you know about Catherine's life,
however, the better you will understand the Little Mandate.

In this connection, I refer you to her autobiography, *Fragments of My Life* (FML), as one companion volume to the present work.

In one sense, Catherine's spiritual life can be seen as the "deeper and deeper" understanding and living out of the meaning of these words of the Mandate spoken by the Lord to her in the depth of her being. My own study of the Mandate has convinced me that these are not "rationally thought out words," but real intuitions of the Spirit. I hope this will become apparent as I present the innumerable ways these same themes are woven together into ever increasing beauty and intricacy. These words are simply "in her," and she does not need to "think them up" each time she wishes to speak. They are in her like the very air she breathes. When she speaks, breath comes out of her mouth. So when she speaks about her spirituality, the words of the Mandate come out of her heart. They are her very life.

Here at the very beginning, in a sort of bird's-eye view of the book, I wish to state these themes, and briefly show how the other lines expand upon them.

> Arise!   Go!   Sell all you possess . . .
>   give it directly, personally, to the poor.
>   Take up My cross (their cross) and follow Me —
>   going to the poor — being poor —
>   being one with them — one with Me.

This first paragraph of the Mandate is its heart; all the other lines are expansion and commentary on the spirituality of these themes.

Life is a journey, a pilgrimage. It is a pilgrimage to union with Christ who is found in the poor. That is, in everyone. In some mysterious way he continues his passion in them. Because of sin and the condition in which we find ourselves, this journey is painful. It necessitates becoming poor, an emptying (kenosis) of the false self, in order to be filled with Christ. Christ emptied himself, became poor for love of us. We can only become united with him now by an inward journey of self-stripping. Thus do we become joined to him in love, which is the goal of human existence.

In the later years of her life Catherine has written whole books on each of these themes. *Strannik* (St) [pilgrim] treats of the journey dimension of human existence. *Urodivoi* (U) [fools for God] deals with divine foolishness, the kenotic aspect of the following of Christ. Her book on poverty is still in manuscript form, but will eventually be published. As we shall see, poverty is not simply one of the virtues for Catherine. It is a way of life, the form which love now must take in our present condition. Finally, *Sobornost* (So) [unity] treats of the total unity of mind and heart with one another which results when Christians empty themselves for the love of the Poor Man. The essential ingredient in all these aspects of the spiritual life — an ingredient which is also a way — is the Cross: without the Cross it is not possible to journey in poverty towards union with the Poor Christ.

> Little — be always little . . . simple —
>   poor — childlike,

Catherine is insistent on calling us to "being before doing." This line concerns the deep characteristics of our being before God. The heart of this line is childlikeness, the call to return to the image of the Divine Child, Jesus. Littleness, simplicity, and total dependence on the Father (spiritual poverty) are the characteristics of the child. These are the states of being without which we cannot unite with the Christ who became poor for love of us. She says that this line is the most difficult of all.

Preach the Gospel WITH YOUR LIFE —
WITHOUT COMPROMISE — listen to
the Spirit — He will lead you.

What are we to do on our journey? Preach the Gospel,
that is, Jesus! We are to manifest, by our lives, the presence
of the risen Christ. The Gospel is a call to the total gift of self
without compromise, since Jesus gave himself totally for us.
"Your Life" means with the totality of the self, using all the
gifts and talents the Lord has given us. It is the Holy Spirit
who will teach us how to do this.

Do little things exceedingly well
for love of Me.

Life is made up of a multitude of little things. Our pride
propels us to make our journey by great leaps and bounds.
No. We are to walk one step at a time, doing everything,
especially the small things, out of great love for Christ.

Love — love — love, never counting
the cost.

Love is the great commandment of the Lord. It occurs in
the center of the seven explanatory lines of the Mandate to
show that it is the center of the Gospel and life. Love of its
nature does not calculate its efforts. Love simply loves.

Go into the market place and stay
with Me . . . pray . . . fast . . .
pray always . . . fast.

The market place is the human heart, where all the
buying and selling takes place. This is a further clarification

also of the "poor": the poor of the first line are not simply the materially poor, but every human being. We are all poor in different ways. The pilgrimage is a journey into the human heart to enrich hearts with the presence of the risen Christ. Prayer and fasting, as Jesus says in the Gospel, are the two great spiritual weapons needed to cast the demons out of the market place of the heart.

> Be hidden — be a light to your neighbor's
> feet. Go without fears into the depth
> of men's hearts . . . I shall be with you.

Most of God's action in the world is hidden: Jesus calls us to walk humbly with our brothers and sisters along their way. The poor and the marketplace, finally, are revealed as the depth of peoples' hearts. In order to enter therein, we must be free of our own fears and anxieties. If we journey into hearts out of love, and in obedience to the Lord's call, we will have the scriptural promise of his constant presence.

> Pray always. I WILL BE YOUR REST.

If we pray always, as the Lord commanded us, we will have the strength to keep walking on our pilgrimage. In a paradoxical way we will know the strength which comes from resting in his arms as we journey. Not only will we rest in God, but in some mysterious fashion Christ will find rest and consolation in us as well.

Catherine is from Russia. Her thought-patterns are circular rather than linear. Hers is not a step by step progression of thought. She is not illogical but alogical, if one may put it that way. Thus in one paragraph, she may express the whole of the Mandate. She is a weaver; the threads of her tapestry are the lines of the Mandate. She does not simply

treat one theme and then pass on to another. All the themes
are present to her all the time.

The present book will reflect something of this thinking. In the West we tend to sort everything out and make a
neat, logical package of a person's life and thought. Even
though I'm trying to accomplish something of this, it really
is not wholly possible. Her thought is too compact, too
intricate. She seeks, by playing the themes over and over
again in a variety of ways, to have them seep into a person's
consciousness and heart. Again, music is a good analogy: the
same lines in a cantata are sung in many different ways.
Likewise, all the themes of the opera may be in the overture.
Catherine can put the whole Mandate in one staff letter, and
sometimes in a short paragraph. Like a good teacher she
repeats her lesson constantly until its message is absorbed.
Thus, there will be this over-lapping of themes. I hope it will
sound in your ears like the music it truly is.

Communal, Ecclesial Words

Perhaps another way to specify the limitations of this
book within the total context of Catherine's teaching is to
make a distinction between personal, and communal or
ecclesial, words. Communal words are the truths of revela-
tion given to us all. The Church is the divinized community
in which we experience them. Catherine's personal spirituality is profoundly and deeply rooted in the truths of the
Gospel, and in the dogmas and sacramental life of the
Church. The Little Mandate concerns her *personal words*,
and this book concerns her *own* spirituality, which by defini-
tion is a particular way of living out the Gospel and the
communal life of the Church. But lest anyone misunder-
stand, and, not knowing Catherine, think of the Little Mandate as some esoteric doctrine cut off from the life of the

Church, it may be well here to emphasize briefly but strongly these ecclesial words which form the context for her life and thought. They are always to be presumed as the basis of her personal life.

The Trinity

In our "Way of Life," or "Constitution," Catherine writes:

> I would like to bring to the family that God has deigned to establish through me the very essence of my spirituality . . . the Trinity . . . which takes its root, of course, from Eastern Spirituality. To me (the Trinity) is a reality of faith. The Trinity is fire, flame, movement. The Trinity dwells within me, I am Its temple. The tips of the wings of the Spirit, in this movement, in this fire, touch the tip of my heart. I appear to be standing in the eye of this fantastic creative movement and fire.
>
> Because this glimpse of the Trinity has been given to me, I know that I am walking on the way that is Christ into the heart of the Father; that I have constant recourse to the Holy Spirit who reminds me of the words of my Brother Jesus Christ, but who also shows me the turns of his way. I know also that when an hour of temptation comes, the mantle of her infinite silence descends upon me and I am confronted by Our Lady of the Trinity. (WL)

The doctrine of the Trinity is the heart of the Christian understanding of life, and thus the essence and starting point of Catherine's. The Ultimate Mystery is a Trinity of Persons. We have come forth from the Trinity, and we shall return. "We have come forth from the Mind of God, and are returning to the Heart of God," is one of her favorite sayings. We are walking the Way (Christ) back into the heart of the Father. It is the Holy Spirit who shows us Jesus the Way and helps us understand his words and life.

> The Eternal Community is the Trinity. It has existed eternally, having no beginning and no end. The Community of Love: God the Father loving the Son, and this love bringing forth the Holy Spirit. (GWC, 55)

Here Catherine points to the Trinity as the model for human existence; we are to become a community of love just as the Trinity is a community of love:

> Yes, this is the very essence of being brought together by the Lord, of being a community moved by Christian love: the incarnation of this gentle, powerful, overwhelming law of God's love into daily loving, into the fabric of our hearts and of our daily lives. In my estimation, then, the primary work of the apostolate is that we love one another. If we implement this law of love, clothe it with flesh, then we shall become Icons of Christ, because people will want from us just the sight of our loving God, ourselves, and one another. (WL)

> In order to form a community of love, man must make contact with the Trinity first. Then and only then can he make a community with his fellowmen. (GWC, 55)

The unity of mind and heart to which Jesus calls us has its source and foundation in the Trinitarian life:

> The Triune God bade us to love. Yes, from the Trinity springs everything that exists, including our hearts that reflect, or rather should reflect, theirs. (St, 39)

Nazareth And The Church

Catherine has a wonderful teaching about this community of love which Madonna House, the Church, and the whole human race should be modelled on, viz. the Trinitarian life. But how can we know what the Trinitarian life is? Her answer to this is *the holy family of Nazareth*:

> It is wonderful to think about the Trinity. It is as if the House of Nazareth opened before our eyes and there was Mary and Joseph and Jesus . . . for these three were also of the same mind and heart.   (S, 39)

I said above that we were dealing here with communal words, the doctrine of the Church which is the context for Catherine's Little Mandate. But I must make an exception for *Nazareth*: Nazareth is more of a personal word for Catherine.

God often attracts founders and foundresses to some specific mystery of the faith. They are immersed, of course, in all the mysteries of the faith, but often one mystery becomes for them a kind of "divine milieu" which pervades, to an unusual degree, their whole life and work. Nazareth is such a mystery for Catherine. No study of her work is complete without it. It is the spiritual atmosphere in which the Little Mandate is lived out. I will treat Nazareth later on.

It is from the holy community of Nazareth that Catherine draws her basic model for life together, viz. family: "Madonna House is the spirit of Nazareth . . . the spirit of a family, the family of Nazareth, the community of perfect charity and love."   (SL #183, 1965)

In the following passage she reveals how the family should be the model for all communities:

For what I am talking about is a deep and beautiful thing. I am not talking only of the best family spirit that could possibly exist in a real blood family, or even amongst ourselves in the natural order (that I desire too), but I am talking about *the family spirit that should be amongst us because we belong to the family of God.*

Consider: God is our Father, Christ our Brother, and the Holy Ghost our Advocate. The Triune God gives us Divine Life and we are truly part of the Divine Family, with Our Lady as our Mother and all the saints as part of the family too. This oneness with the Divine Family, with the Church Triumphant, with Our Lady, should be reflected in each one of us. We should love one another as God the Father loves His Son, so that from our love for one another the Holy Spirit would also become visible to those around us.   (SL #119, 1962)

The Divine Family here is the Church. Our Lady is its Mother. It is divine because it is filled with the divine life of the Holy Spirit. And just as the Spirit is the love of Father and Son, so our love for one another should be so intense that the Spirit is almost palpable to those around us.

The Church

After the section on the Trinity in our "Way of Life," there follows the section on the Church:

We are a family within the great family of God which is Christ's Holy Catholic Church. We rejoice in our membership in the Church, and cherish our communion with the Pope and all the bishops, especially our own, wherever we may be, and with all our brethren in the faith, of every nation and age. We proclaim no other Gospel than that which all these faithful witnesses of Christ and His Church believe and teach. (WL)

Catherine's love, understanding, and devotion to the Church is extraordinary, and no superlatives would do it justice. From her Eastern Tradition she received the understanding that the Church is *even now* the Bride of Christ, the Body of Christ, the community divinized by the Spirit. We tend, especially in modern times, to emphasize the "not yet" aspect of the Church, its humanness, its "unlikeness" to God, rather than its deep nature of *already being now* the Spotless Bride. As Catherine's life proceeded, she was led deeper and deeper into this realization:

As I grew up I began to understand the Christian idea of the Church. At some point, somewhere along the line, I realized who and what the Church was. I was young. I was in England, and I read something. Suddenly, like a flash, I realized that She was the Spotless Bride of Christ. I saw her clad in the King's robes, beautiful and glorious. This vision stayed in my heart like a warm, consoling thought: the Church was the Bride of Christ, spotless, without blemish, shining, radiant. As scripture says, "The King's daughter is decked in her chamber with gold-woven robes; in many colored robes she is led to the King" (Ps 45: 13-14). Yes, my imagination was working overtime. I know that she wasn't clad with just anything, She was something so holy, so precious, something you should die for. This is the Church.

Yes, I understood. I understood the Mystical notion of the nuptials of the Christian with his God. I cannot explain it. It's beyond explanation. But because I entered into the mystery of love which is God, I entered into the mystery of His Church which is His beloved; and I still live in this mystery.

When such things happen to people, then the Church as a mystery, the Church as the Bride, the Church as the People of God, the Church as the Mystical Body of Christ, becomes a reality of faith, for we are in the realm of faith. (CI)

Catherine's intense love for the Church is revealed in the following prophetic cry against those who lack faith in the Church's deep, inner reality and sanctity as the Bride of Christ. Catherine often read this poem to us:

Howl, my soul, howl,
Cry to the Lord for His Church,
Howl, my soul, howl.

Look! See how she is torn asunder!
How her members mock and ridicule her,
Laughing their hellish laughter
As they trample her into the mire of their
twisted souls!

Howl, my soul, howl before the Lord,
As tortured men howled on medieval racks!
For those who are Thy people
Are trying to make a harlot of Thy Bride!

Howl, my soul, howl,
For the Church is in pain.
Look, she lies in the dust of a thousand roads.
No one stops; the Good Samaritan is not seen
At the bend of those roads yet!   (JI, I)

Catherine will often use the image of the Good Samaritan. Here, the Christian is called to lift the whole Church, as well as individuals, out of the ditch, and pour the oil of love and the wine of compassion on her wounds.

The Church and her sacraments, and especially the Eucharist, is where we receive the love to restore the icon of the Trinity in our own hearts and in every family:

> Before Jesus ascended into heaven, he gave us the Church. He wouldn't leave us orphans. At that time he also gave to men another mystery, the mystery that keeps the Church alive. It is the mystery of the Eucharist. The simplest thing that a man could give is bread and wine. He made them a vehicle of his love, a vehicle of his strength, the strength of a Christian to live his law of love. It is there, in the mystery of the Eucharist, that we get the strength to live the law of love. (CI)

Mary

The Trinity — Father, Son, and Holy Spirit — is the Ultimate Mystery, and the Church is the earthly manifestation of the Community of the Divine Life. Next in importance for Catherine is the person who, after Church, was the most perfect manifestation of the restoration of the divine image among us, viz. Mary, the Theotokos, the Mother of God. The importance and significance of Mary is constantly woven throughout all of Catherine's teachings.

You will recall that in her remarks above on the Trinity, Our Lady of the Trinity was also present. Mary is all-pervasive in Catherine's thinking and life. I cite here a passage from one of our most treasured documents, a talk Catherine gave in 1956 on the "Spirit of the Madonna House Apostolate." It sums up perfectly what, for lack of space, cannot be elaborated more fully:

To me it is self-evident that he who seeks Christ without Mary seeks him in vain. All the things that I have just spoken to you presuppose the Way to the Father (who is Christ, for he said, "I am the Way"), but the gate to the Way is Mary. And we are *Domus Dominae*, the home of Mary, Madonna House. Should one have to mention the self-evident? All the things I spoke about will happen to you, if you go to Jesus through Mary. She possesses the secret of prayer, the secret of wisdom, for she is the Mother of God. Who else can teach you to burn with the fire of love except the Mother of fair love? Who else can teach you to pray, except the woman of prayer? Who else can teach you to go through the silence of deserts and nights, the silence of pain and sorrow, the silence of joy and gladness, except the woman rapt in silence?

Who can span the bridge between the 'old you' and the 'new you,' you the undedicated one, and you the dedicated one? Only Mary! She is the bridge between the Old Testament and the New, the Jewish girl who brought forth the Messiah, the Son of the Almighty.

Sometimes it is difficult to speak of the self-evident. Without Mary, how can one speak of God the Father who was so well-pleased with her that he made her the mother of his son? How can one speak of Christ who was her son, begotten by the Holy Spirit, without speaking of Mary, the Spouse of the Holy Spirit? Our Lady of the Trinity, Our Lady of Madonna House, are one and the same. All of us are consecrated to her. That's why we are free. That is why we can dedicate ourselves so utterly to her Son, because she will show us the way. (SMHA)*

This devotion to Mary is not, for Catherine, some optional pious practice. Mary's all-pervasive presence is deeply

---

* The complete talk is given in the Appendix. In my opinion it is the most prophetic statement Catherine ever made on the inner spirit of Madonna House.

rooted in the Church's understanding of the Mystery of Redemption. As Mother of Christ, Mother of God, Mother of the Church, she is the Mother of all Christians. Devotion to her is not optional for the true Christian. And there can be no complete Spirit of Nazareth without her presence. What would a home, a family, be, without the presence of a mother?

Thus, from the doctrine of the Trinity, Catherine derives her understanding of Church and community. And community derives its nature from the *home* of Nazareth, which is the basic model for all Christians, for the whole human race, the best earthly icon of the Trinity.

Nicolas Zernov, in *The Russians and Their Church*, describes this movement in the Russian spirit towards community and family thus:

> Russia's special genius was the art of Christian living, the application of Christianity to the corporate daily life of the people. And here her contribution was of the first importance. Her ideal was that of a Christian State living as one family, in which every person, from the Sovereign down to the poorest and least educated of its members, could have his full share of spiritual benefits and joys. The sense of being one community experienced by the Russians was spontaneous and organic. It arose not from obedience to authority, nor from the idea of duty, nor from intellectual agreement: it was due to a pattern of life, a rhythm of existence which was lovingly designed, built and followed by the entire population. Innumerable Church customs and home traditions provided the content of that ritual of daily life which was the most distinctive mark of Russian culture.

The Beatitudes

The Beatitudes are quoted in full in our "Way of Life." This is because Catherine sees the Beatitudes as a summary of the Gospel; in several places she also equates her Little Mandate with the Beatitudes:

> On a piece of yellow paper I had typed what we call today our Mandate. I read it again and again. I looked at it with eyes touched, in a manner of speaking, by the finger of God. It was as if I were a blind man and he was restoring my sight! It seemed to me that he was leading me by the hand to the very essence of his Heart. And right next to the yellow paper on which I had typed the Mandate . . . I kept reading the Beatitudes. (She quotes them). In a sense, the Mandate and the Beatitudes came so close together in my heart that they blended into one another. (SLFF #80, 1977)

I think it's true to say that the Beatitudes are the biblical *locus* for Catherine's spirituality. The Mandate is her personally inspired way of living out this new way of life described by Jesus: "So in the end I knew what I had to do. I had to sell all I possessed, give it to the poor, and be poor for their sake, for his sake. The first paragraph of our Mandate is, in a sense, the Beatitudes." (SLFF #80)

Faith

There is no virtue which Catherine emphasizes as much as faith. Without it there can be no love: "Faith is the cradle of hope and love." Dorothy Day said of Catherine that "she has the gift of a great and joyous faith and of making life an adventure, a pilgrimage." St. Paul speaks of the charism of faith. This is not simply the gift of faith of the ordinary believer. It is the possession of an overwhelming faith which is capable of inspiring faith in others. Catherine has this gift to a remarkable degree. She never ceases to call people to deeper faith as the foundation of the whole Christian life. Of the countless passages I could quote from her works, the following will lead us naturally into the first line of the Mandate. Here she speaks of faith as a pilgrimage:

> Faith is a pilgrimage towards the Absolute. Faith gives every Christian sandals and a pilgrim's staff and bids him to arise and go in search of him whom every Christian longs for — God.
>
> Faith appears to be blind sometimes but in reality it sees very deeply. It alone can walk in utter darkness. It alone can fold the wings of the intellect when necessary and open them when it needs to. Chasms, abysses, steep mountains present no problems or difficulty to faith. On the contrary, all of life — the pains, sorrows, joys, symbolized by these chasms — becomes its food and its nourishment. Faith grows until it leaves all darkness behind and walks like a child bathed in the light of God's love.   (GWC, 128)

This is a perfect introduction to the Mandate. We are about to follow Catherine as she describes the journey to the lonely Christ. Faith is our guide on this journey. We walk as children bathed in God's love. Let us begin.

CHAPTER TWO

Arise! Go!

* * *

In an early presentation of the Little Mandate to the community, Catherine quotes the first paragraph of the Mandate, and then she says:

> This is the original message that pursued me through several years. 'Pursued' is the word. It would not leave me alone! Accompanying it was a deep, inner unshakable conviction that this arising, this going, this journey, was a journey to *Bethlehem*, but that my life would be spent in Nazareth . . . I'm trying to simply render here the few ideas, graces, words, that I consider are God's Words to me. Next, when God's will seemed to lead me from the obscurity of Nazareth into the market place, I did not understand, I just went. (SL #204, 1966)

She called this letter "The Mandate of God to Catherine." "It doesn't occupy much space on a piece of paper, but that's all I have to give you, that's all God gave me personally, and that is what I have lived for. That is, to me, all that matters, for it is to me the soul, the heart, of the Apostolate." (SL #204)

"Bethlehem" is Catherine's symbol for spiritual child-hood, the restoration of the divine image. We shall take it up in the second line of the Mandate. We are interested here in the journey aspect of her thinking: "I just went."

At a community meeting in 1969 she said:

> This "arise and go" is something in us at every mo-ment. It is something so deep, so profound, so constantly challenging. It is a Voice calling to us, the Voice of God. We can plug our ears; we can plead sickness; we can plead ignorance; we can plead sinfulness — anything and every-thing because unconsciously we're afraid to go.
>
> Like Abraham we don't know where we are going — and we don't want to know! That's really the essence of the words 'arise and go!' The Voice doesn't say where we are going, but we are going to the poor, that is, the whole earth.   (Unpublished Talk)

"The Mandate of God to Catherine" implies a call, a *vocation*. This is the first element in Catherine's thinking about "arise and go." It is like Abraham's call in that he did not know where he was going. He was simply told to break camp and travel west. The Abraham cycle from Genesis 12 is the earliest strata of the Old Testament. One of the deepest and most ancient of words of God to his people is, therefore, "Go forth from the land of your kinsfolk and from your father's house to a land that I will show you" (Gn 12:1).

It is typical of authentic words of God that they are not fully explained. God tells people to do something and to trust that he will be with them. He doesn't spell out all the details. He does not explain everything that is going to happen. He does not tell you where you are going or what it is going to cost. Implicit in the command is the assurance of his presence, help, and guidance. Only by moving and journeying will these latter become a reality, not before.

Catherine had "some" word from God where she was going: she was going to the poor, that is, to everyone, into human hearts.

So that is the first dimension of "Arise! Go!" It is the Voice of God calling us to participate in his plan of salvation history.

The second dimension is pilgrimage, that life itself is a journey, movement. You will recall that, for Catherine, the life of the Trinity is fire and movement, a movement towards God. Her favorite words for this are journey and pilgrimage. She entitled her whole collection of privately published poetry *Journey Inward*. For the Introduction she wrote:

> Our journey of life . . . should be a journey inward, to meet the God who dwells within us. It is a long journey, not in time, perhaps, but in effort. It is a journey of death, yet of life . . . a journey of strife that leads to peace, of pain that leads to healing, of sorrow that turns into joy. (JI, I)

Human existence is a journey inward undertaken out of a passionate desire to make Christ known and loved, and to become one with the indwelling Trinity. Faith seeks to rip apart the curtains separating one from the Beloved. *Strannik* is her most comprehensive elaboration of "Arise! Go!"

The "Arise! Go!" within us is a nostalgia for paradise:

> I wonder what happened to Adam and Eve when they left the garden? They didn't know it but they had been given another paradise. Adam and Eve embarked on a pilgrimage with a nostalgia for what had been. The audible, visible presence of God, his friendship, was like a fire . . . in the hearts of Adam and Eve. They were the first pilgrims of the Absolute . . . because they had known the Absolute . . . and this knowledge passed into the hearts of all their children. (St 9, 10)

In one of her poems Catherine calls herself a pilgrim of the Absolute since she is a child of Adam and Eve:

I am a pilgrim of the Absolute
A strange, unnoticed pilgrim
Who walks, yet always somehow
stands still.   (JI, 1)

Christ Is The Supreme Pilgrim:

Christ was the total pilgrim, the man
who pilgrimaged from the bosom of his Father
to the hearts of men.   (St 13)

Yes, Christ was the Supreme Pilgrim, the incredible
Pilgrim who descended from heaven to earth and
returned from earth to heaven, thereby making us free.
(St 14)

Christ The Pilgrim

I seem to be a pilgrim on this earth!
A pilgrim poor who has nowhere to lay his head.
And has to beg for his crust of bread.
A beggar whose voice is low, unheard by many.   (JI, 1)

Christ, as a Beggar of love who roams the world seeking love, is one of Catherine's favorite themes. The Russians have a legend that Christ anonymously wanders throughout Russia seeking love. Catherine also is a beggar walking with the Beggar of Love:

The Song Of A Pilgrim

I am a lonely pilgrim with empty hands,
I beg my way from land to land.

I am a beggar of the Lord.
I cannot rest because I must show the face of
God from place to place and witnesss to him
to all I meet.

The Lord has given me the grace of restless feet and
a hungry heart. I cannot rest because I must follow
my Love as he walks the earth, a Beggar of Love.
I am the pilgrim who walks with him. (JI, 1)

Jesus came to set us free, to give us the freedom to walk
on a pilgrimage of love toward the Father:

Free to undertake a pilgrimage of love.
There is no denying that every Christian
must make a pilgrimage of love. He enters
into the pilgrimage of love to the Father,
to God. He has to walk that long road
inward, take that journey, that pilgrimage
inward, that alone will make him touch
Christ who dwells within. (St 14)

We are on a pilgrimage into the Trinity, into the poor,
into the marketplace, and the marketplace is the hearts of
men. Such a journey will of necessity be painful:

When I read and re-read the Little Mandate . . . I
suddenly knew why my feet were bloody: I was going into
the depths of men's hearts. That is a precipitous pilgrimage. The depths are stony and they wound your feet. It is a
precipitous descent because men's hearts are deep; it is
taking the pain of men upon yourself. It was the carrying
of another man's cross. Such a pilgrimage can be undertaken only with love, and not with any ordinary love.
Human love does not want precipitous descents into
men's hearts. (St 51-52)

One of Catherine's key ideas reflected in the above is identification, (which we shall treat later): God identified himself with us in the Incarnation. Our pilgrimage is also a journey into identification with others, and thus with God:

> He has to enter the hearts of men, and the only way to enter, the only key that allows men to enter the hearts of others, is *identifying* oneself with the other. This identification is excruciating. It takes faith to identify oneself with the other.

> The next step does not happpen to many. It happens to a few, for the Lord is merciful. Now the pilgrim faces a very simple thing, for God speaks to him of a total identification with Himself. He presents him with the sight of a cross on which he will have to lie, and on which he will have to be crucified. This is, as far as the pilgrim knows, the goal to which he is led.   (St 64-65)

Pilgrims "pray all the time" and finally come to rest in the heart of God:

> So the pilgrim comes to a point where he has to rest, not in the depths of men's heart, but in the heart of God. He has to listen to the heartbeats of God. The Lord in his immense goodness and mercy lifts a little corner of his own mystery so that the pilgrim can really preach him in the marketplace, so that he can really become a Gospel, so that he can really become fire and flame and light! (St 80)

Strannik is a marvelous example of the explication of the whole Mandate in terms of one of its themes. In the few quotations I have presented we have the whole tapestry of the Mandate: We are on a journey into God, into Christ, into the hearts of men. It is painful. The way is identification with them, which demands a stripping of all that is not God.

We pray as we go until we reach our own crucifixion. Then we become walking Gospels, incarnations of the light and flame and fire of the Trinity. The final stage is "becoming the friend of God":

> He stands in the market place radiating more and more fire, but he does not know it. He is steeped in joy, humility of heart, and docility. He becomes a child. He belongs to Bethlehem and Nazareth. The impact of his life is fantastic. He constantly reproduces in his life the Incarnation, the suffering, the death, and the resurrection of the Lord.   (St 83-84)

The spirit of pilgrimage is deeply ingrained in the soul of the Russian people. The first chapter in Arseniev's *Russian Piety* is entitled, "Nostalgia for Space." The immensity of their land has a counter-part in an experience of inner immensity, the vastness of interior space:

> Sometimes buffeted to extremes, full of burning faith, the troubled soul would find in these places (of pilgrimage) the peace and spiritual comfort which it needed. In this way a kind of aesthetic of pilgrimage evolved: the joyous transformation of nature and the wandering life through a spiritual experience . . . and a certain spirit of adventure.   (18)

"Aesthetic of pilgrimage" is a pointer to a profound dimension of Catherine's spirituality. We saw above that one aspect of the Russian genius is the application of the Gospel to every dimension of life. The pilgrimage into the hearts of our brothers and sisters is simultaneously a beatification of the world: the image of God now shines through the face of people as they use all created things to glorify the Creator. As the pilgrim travels he creates beauty:

They were profoundly convinced that this world, notwithstanding its imperfection, was intended to become the glorious temple of the Holy Spirit, and that man was empowered by God to be the chief agent in the process of transfiguration. Man, through his love and free obedience to the Incarnate Lord, could revive and restore the shining beauty of the Divine Image within himself and restore harmony and peace in the world around him.   (107)

When Catherine was a young girl she desired to make a pilgrimage:

I was a very mischievous child and always in hot water of some kind. One day I read a story of a young woman going on a pilgrimage; I decided to go on a pilgrimage myself. So I collected a long black skirt some place, a big black shawl, and an icon, and off I went through the streets of Petrograd. I must have looked funny, for quite a few people turned around and looked at me. I reached the outskirts of Petrograd and was on my way to a country road when the police found me. I must have been conspicuous. Anyhow, I was returned to my parents. Nobody upbraided me or anything, but father said: "Well, number one, you should have asked permission — mother's and mine; or at least you should have had the charity to leave a little note as to where you were going." And that ended the episode. But in my mind it remained as unfinished business. In my early twenties this picture kept coming back to mind, and I entitled it, "Unfinished Pilgrimage." (HMCB)

Adventure

The spirit behind this early pilgrimage is nothing as heavy or profound as a "journey into the hearts of men." Rather, it was the spirit of adventure, of exploration into

God and the vastness of God's world. Never think that Catherine's journey is all pain and seriousness! The following poem (which she loved but which was not written by her) is an insight into this adventurous, almost playful, aspect of her pilgrimaging heart:

Against Peace

Ask for danger
Ask for glory
the fear and the fun
And life — like a story
In the wind and the sun.

Send us now
A sudden waking
A royal row
A thorough shaking

Pray you Lord,
At the end of writing,
Send us a sword
And a little fighting.

Send us danger,
Send us glory
the fear and the fun —
And death like a story
In the wind and the sun.   (JI, I)

Holy Restlessness

There is a holy restlessness about Catherine which is connected to her pilgrim spirit. She is never satisfied either with herself or others! We can always love God more, and restore his world more completely to him:

Arise, arise, stop being sleepy! Stop being blah, blah, blah! Stop it! In the dark of the night, in the reality of everyday living, God says, "Arise! Enough sleeping!" Listen carefully to the whisper of the wind, the Word of the Lord: "Arise, arise, come! Come up higher," says Christ. Arise contains the notion of movement. You cannot stand still. The word "Arise" wakes you up. (LDM, 1980)

One of Catherine's most frequently quoted sayings from the Gospel is, "Friend, come up higher." We of Madonna House heard her say that hundreds of times. It is Christ calling his friends to the adventure of love, the pilgrimage towards the Absolute, the journey into the hearts of ourselves and others.

Journey To Nazareth

I introduced the theme of Nazareth above, and I said that it is the mystery of the life of Christ which has a very special personal significance for Catherine and those called to her community. I wish now to develop this most important aspect of her spirituality. The journey that she is on is, in a most special way, a journey to Nazareth:

Nazareth And I

At Mass all fell away from me as if it never was. I stood before myself beholding the ragged clothing of my life. I could not understand why I wasn't naked, but I was not.

No, I was clothed as I had been once before in rough gray linen tied at the waist with a simple string. Across my shoulder was a linen bag; in it was black bread and salt. Across the other shoulder a gourd filled with clear water hung easily. In my hand I had some sort of sturdy stick.

A voice said clearly: "Arise again and go, a healing, consoling, blessing, loving, without many knowing or realizing. For you are entering the hiddenness of Nazareth. You see, your passion has already ended. Now you begin again." (JI, II, 1970)

I give the date of this poem because I am going to take you on a little journey of Catherine's growing awareness of the significance of Nazareth. And as I speak of the great significance of this mystery for her, I am not trying to arrange it in any theological order of importance with the other mysteries. The Spirit can and often does attract founders and foundresses to one particular mystery which becomes the doorway to Christ, the motivating force behind their other virtues, the spiritual atmosphere in which their lives are lived out. It is the mystery which gives a characteristic stamp to their whole thought and being. Nazareth is such a mystery for Catherine, and I believe this can be easily shown from her writings.

What I wish to do here, then, is emphasize the *centrality* and *importance* of Nazareth. What it *means* will be shown as we go through the Mandate. Nazareth is one of the major harmonies which flows through the music of her whole life.

The overwhelming significance of Nazareth for Catherine is revealed in the very first lines of our "Way of Life." This is the major document Catherine has left her community as a guide for the future. It begins thus:

God works in strange ways! When I first put together on a piece of paper what we today call the 'Little Mandate,' which begins with the words, "Arise! Go! Sell all you

possess . . ." upon reading it over again and again, I
thought that God was calling me to Nazareth. To me,
Nazareth was the Little Mandate and the Little Mandate
was Nazareth. (WL)

Catherine equates the Mandate with *no other mystery of
Christ's life.* To repeat: it is not a question of importance in a
theological scale of values, but of a mystery which the Holy
Spirit wishes to be the "divine milieu" of her vocation.

Catherine has written several volumes called *The History
of the Apostolate.* In the first volume she describes what the
Holy Spirit was doing in her heart prior to her going to the
slums to live with the poor:

> During the year preceeding my visit to the Ordinary of
> Toronto, I made a pilgrimage of priests, as you know. At
> the same time, I was tremendously drawn to the reading
> of the Scriptures, especially the New Testament; and my
> mind constantly dwelt with Nazareth.   (18)
>
> I thought of the slums as Nazareth. (20) And Nazareth
> meant to me a School of Love to which I had to go, if I
> were to do what my heart seemingly wanted so much to
> do, namely, restore the world to Christ.   (21)
>
> I could not think of any better school of love or charity,
> than to dwell in Nazareth.   (22)
>
> My meditations on Nazareth lasted for ten years. . . In
> the early days of Friendship House all my writings re-
> flected this attraction to Nazareth. (22) My vocation was to
> love, and I had to go to Nazareth to learn to love. (23)

In her extraordinary tape on the origins of the Mandate
she says:

I understood that by going to my Bethlehem, my Nazareth, by identifying myself with the poor, by living their life, by living the Gospel without compromise, by loving always, by remaining little, I would be hidden as Christ was hidden in Nazareth. And I considered Nazareth at the same time, as the be-all and center of my vocation.   (HMCB)

You see the magnitude of the mystery of Nazareth in her eyes: it was the "be-all, end-all, center of my vocation"! It is not just another mystery. In some of her early writings she often puts Bethlehem and Nazareth together in such phrases as "let us enter the school of Bethlehem and Nazareth . . . making our home in Bethlehem and Nazareth." But I believe it's clear that Bethlehem has much less significance for her as a *way of life*. Bethlehem is her symbol for a state of being, and especially spiritual childhood. But Nazareth is a *whole way of life*, affecting *how* we express the divine life.

There *is* a sense, however, in which Bethlehem is in a deeper sense the *goal* of the pilgrimage, whereas Nazareth is more the *way*.

Consider one of Catherine's most profound statements about our Madonna House way of life:

For us to live in Nazareth we must, strange as it may seem, begin with Golgotha and the tomb! Then, resurrected in him, by his grace, we shall journey to Bethlehem with the knowledge of the resurrected Christ, and live in Nazareth in expectation of the parousia.   (SL #183)

This was written in 1965. My interpretation of this profound passage is that we are on a kind of reverse pilgrimage from that of the Lord. Through faith and baptism we, by grace, immediately share the resurrected life. But for that life to restore fully the shattered image and likeness of God in us, we must travel backwards through all the mysteries of the Christ-life. Born from the tomb and Calvary, we travel through the public life — transfigurations and healings and struggles — back to Nazareth and on to Bethlehem. Personally for Catherine and her spiritual children, Nazareth is much more the over-riding mystery.

But Nazareth is not the goal. The goal is spiritual rebirth into the fullness of our divine childhood. This is Bethlehem. For just as we were born from the side of Christ on the cross, so the cross, for Christ, becomes his Bethlehem, the place where, as the Father's perfect Child, he made his greatest earthly act of acceptance of the Father's will:

The Fourteenth Station Of The Cross

The Tomb became Manger again,
birthplace of life.
When it received the Lord of life,
Lifeless, dead! (SC)

It would take us too far afield to explore the Russian background of Catherine's vision of the slums as Nazareth. It will be sufficient to point out here that her own mother often went, accompanied by Catherine, "to the people," a rich person going to the poor to minister to them in the name of Christ. This is a characteristic of Russian spirituality:

There were cases of the renunciation of high social rank, family, fortune; but without entrance into the monastic life, for this (latter) was the rejection of all forms of life accepted and venerated by the world. There were

then cases of total renunciation, where the holder of an
honored position would descend to the bottom of the
social scale (so clearly stratified in Russia) and mix with the
simple people, with the poor among the non-privileged
classes, and would become one of them, even poorer than
they, having no home, no means, no family, no position,
however modest.   (*Russian Piety*, 107-108)

In 1825 Czar Alexander I disappeared from his throne.
In 1864, in Siberia, a certain Fedor Kuzmich, past the age of
eighty, died. He was an extremely cultured man who lived
such a life among the peasants. Scholars still cannot agree on
whether it was the Czar or not, but many Russian people
believed that he was.

Also, in the latter part of the 19th century, there was the
whole "populist movement" in Russia where thousands of
people literally left their cultured existence and went to live
among the poor. Many of these were of the "intelligentsia."
They may not have been motivated by conscious gospel
values, but they were following some deep instinct in the
Russian psyche.

We have a collection of letters which Catherine wrote to
her spiritual director, Fr. Paul Furfey, while she was in
Harlem. In 1941 she wrote:

I think much lately of Christ's hidden life. There is
within it, hidden somewhere deeply out of my sight, a
pattern for our Lay Apostolate. Again and again my
thoughts come back to that strange unknown time of his.
One thought especially fascinates me: Identification with
the poor. I am like a moth around a candle. Within that
word "identification" I sense a whole way of life. At times I
catch something of it, and then the veil falls down again.
(FL)

We shall treat of identification shortly. The growing awareness here is that Nazareth is beginning to assume the importance of "a pattern for the Lay Apostolate," "a whole way of life." I believe Combermere is the full flowering of what was, in 1941, a dim vision on her spiritual horizon.

I have mentioned several fundamental documents from Catherine which express the very foundations of our life: our "Way of life," a tape on "The Spirit of Madonna House," another tape on "How the Little Mandate Came to Be," and several others. But if I was asked what is the most important *Staff Letter* she ever wrote, my choice would be May 18, 1965, #183. She went into the poustinia from May 10 to May 15, precisely to ask for a "further clarification of GOD'S MANDATE TO ME." Thus the letter flows out of an intense period of prayer and reflection, after which she articulated what she saw as the essence of Madonna House and the way of life the Spirit had inspired her to follow. I've decided to quote practically the entire letter. It is the best short summary of the Mandate in terms of the Mandate's most central theme, Nazareth. I will also then be able to refer back to this letter as we continue our journey:

> I was now, this May, 1965, in the poustinia, praying to the Lord to further clarify this Mandate to me so that I could, in turn, try to clarify it to you, as so many of you desire me to do. So with a prayer to the Holy Spirit, I will now try to do so.
>
> MADONNA HOUSE IS THE SPIRIT
>   OF NAZARETH.
> MADONNA HOUSE SPIRIT IS THAT OF
>   A FAMILY.
> MADONNA HOUSE SPIRIT IS THAT OF
>   A FAMILY —
> THE FAMILY OF NAZARETH — WHICH WAS
>   'A COMMUNITY OF PERFECT CHARITY AND LOVE.'

These three points go together. Let us see. The spirit of Nazareth? Of course, first and foremost, it is *charity*. Even before Christ's birth there existed between Joseph and Mary a great and sublime love. These two were already a "community of charity." Moreover, I believe God arranged that Madonna House — the child of Friendship House — would be a replica of this type of love, this community of charity. For, contrary to all the existing norms of the day, and almost from the first day of our formation and foundation of Friendship House, he brought men and women, Mary and Joseph, to live in chastity, even as did Mary and Joseph. They loved each other perfectly, and in many ways. As the years go by we must pray over, meditate upon, and understand better and better this beautiful facet of the mystery of Nazareth.

Another facet, in connection with the above, that comes to me often when I meditate on God's Mandate to me is the pregnancy of Mary. She was already pregnant with God before the family, the community of love between her and Joseph, was established.

Each person who comes to the Madonna House is, in a manner of speaking — or should be — "pregnant with God." Those who are not do not have a vocation to Madonna House. This "pregnancy" is a grace from God himself. He gives them a desire for himself. This becomes a "seed" within them, leading them to Mary and Joseph's Nazareth — Madonna House — there to dwell in hiddenness, humility, hard work at little, daily tasks (which, if performed with great love would truly preach the Gospel loudly!)

There are many places he could have led them: the vast deserts of the contemplative Orders, the rocky but beautiful, steep road of married life, the heights of priestly life, or that of the active religious Orders. And maybe each one called to these various vocations would have to go to

Nazareth — but not in the way of the Madonna House Mandate. For our Apostolate, Nazareth seems to be a very permanent place, spiritually speaking. Even Eddie and I have been led very mysteriously to live there like Mary and Joseph.

So, pregnant with Christ, chosen by him, led by him, people are brought to the Nazareth of Madonna House to give birth to him and to allow him to grow to his full stature. They live with the Holy Family, as Jesus lived with Mary and Joseph for many years.

The next point that came to me in my meditation was the extent of the Holy Family's *identification with the villagers*. The Holy Family formed part and parcel of the familiar landscape. They spoke the same language. They had the same status, or, perhaps even a lower one than some of the other villagers, for didn't they say, "Isn't this just the carpenter's son?"

This too is in the Mandate of God to us — that we blend and identify ourselves with those we serve, as much as it is humanly possible. Especially with the poor. If, as may happen, on rare occasion, we are called to serve "the rich poor," then even moreso we bring to them Nazareth and everything it stands for: the community of love, poverty, simplicity, hard work, joy.

There is no denying that Mary, God's Mother, was a contemplative. First and foremost she was always before God. She lived in the presence of God the Father, God the Holy Spirit who overshadowed her, and God the Son who was bodily within her!

Yet she worked for the Lord too, serving the needs of Joseph and Jesus, and I am certain, of many, many, of the villagers, and of the pilgrims and strangers passing by. Maybe she served just by listening and gently advising those in trouble and sorrow; by sharing her food; by general hospitality; by many other simple and direct ways which today we call the spiritual and corporal works of mercy.

Joseph likewise was a contemplative. How could he be anything else? He lived with God and God's Mother. He was a silent man, a man evidently of deep prayer. Yet, we feel sure that he too "worked for the Lord," first by being a provider for his own family, and then by assisting his neighbors. He probably not only did things for them but counseled them also at the gates with the elders. Here, in these two, Mary and Joseph, I see so clearly the spirit and techniques of Madonna House.

As for Christ himself, *being* before his Father was his very life, its essence. God the Father chose for Christ his earthly parents, and Christ accepted them lovingly all his life, from the cave of Bethlehem, through many years of manual labor in the hidden life, throughout his whole ministry, passion, death, and resurrection. *In all things he hastened to do the will of his Father.*

Our Madonna House life should be like that. For us, the will of the Father is revealed by the needs of the Apostolate at every given moment of our day. It seems so simple!

How do we preach the Gospel with our lives? Again, we look at the Holy Family. They lived the law without compromise, for Christ came to fulfill the law, not to abolish it. But he gave us a new law in the New Alliance, and it is that new law that we have to live without compromise, just as the Holy Family lived the will of the Father in the Old Law without compromise.

Our poverty should be the poverty of Nazareth and the Holy Family. They were artisans. They had enough to keep body and soul together. They lived simple, uncomplicated lives. They were not destitute, but obviously they had none of the luxuries of the day. (In fact they probably would have been eligible for government aid as being below the poverty level.)

But their poverty was luminous, because they were utterly detached from their wills and attached to the will of God the Father. It was utterly complete! There is an endless wealth of meditation here; and parallels for our Madonna House life and spirit abound!

Nazareth is our model, our spiritual home. It is a community of love, of *caritas*, poor, detached from self and self-will, totally attached to God's will. We are engaged in an ordinary life, seemingly simple, unadventurous, monotonous, a life of daily tasks done with great love for God and neighbor! In this way we become witnesses to God. It has been said that to be a witness of God does not consist in engaging in propaganda, nor in stirring people up, but in being a living mystery. It means "to live in such a way that one's life would not make sense if God did not exist." That is what I mean when I say that the Spirit of Madonna House and its Apostolate is one of *witnessing to God before men.*

We must be preachers of the Gospel with our lives — with our words also, when required — but especially with our lives, without compromise, in the market places of the world. Madonna House, therefore, is a group of people called by God himself to give him birth in this particular Nazareth of our modern market place. There we must show him to those who dwell around us *by our lives*!

All this is simple, but not easy! It presupposes death to self, kenosis, violence to oneself, for "heaven is taken by violence!" It's a loving, gentle violence to one's self for the love of God with whom we desire to spend both this life and eternity.

Yes, this is the proviso to all I have written above. The Lord showed it to me from the very beginning of the Apostolate. He showed it to me gently but vividly, showed it to me not only for myself, but for all those whom he has called to Madonna House, to give him birth, and to allow him to grow to his full stature.

This is the proviso, the special accent, the way, the means: *for us to live in Nazareth we must begin with Golgotha and the tomb!* Then, resurrected in him, and by his grace, we shall journey to Bethlehem with the knowledge of the resurrected Christ, and live in Nazareth in expectation of the parousia. Possessing this grace, we shall understand how to do God's will perfectly.

These are the thoughts that came to me in the great silence of God in the poustinia at Marian Meadows in May, 1965. Humbly and lovingly I share them with you in the hope that our Lady of Nazareth and of Combermere will explain these thoughts in all their fullness. (SL #183, 1965)

The Whole Mandate is here — love, poverty, identification with the poor, hiddenness, kenosis, prayer, preaching the Gospel with one's life, doing simple, humble tasks for others, the cross. We shall treat each of these themes more extensively in the other lines of the Mandate. As I develop these themes I hope to show how Catherine relates them all to Nazareth, since this is the permanent spiritual place where the Mandate is lived out.

CHAPTER THREE

Poverty

* * *

Sell all you possess . . .
give it directly,
personally, to the poor . . .
going to the poor . . .
being poor . . .

Having treated the theme of pilgrimage we proceed to Catherine's teaching on poverty and the poor. The supreme goal of Catherine's pilgrimage is to meet the suffering Christ in the poor, there to pour ointment on his wounds, dry his tears, and console him in his loneliness.

The command to "be poor" appears also in the second line of the Mandate. Catherine comments: "So, at this point, two ideas of poverty were working themselves out in my soul: one physical and geographical; the other transcendent and difficult to grasp."   (HMCB)

By this she means that "poor" in the first line really refers to *physical poverty*, the actual giving away of all one possesses. It is the only phrase of the Mandate which does not have universal application but applies specifically to Catherine and to those in the community she has founded (or to anyone else who may be led by the Spirit along this path).

"Sell all you possess" can, of course, be interpreted in a spiritual sense, and Catherine herself will often speak of it in this way. But it should be clear that its primary meaning in the first line refers to physical-material poverty.

Since this is so, I am not going to develop too extensively her teaching on material poverty; much of it would only apply to those called to live on the providence of God in some radical way.

I will begin this section on poverty with a brief treatment of   (1) begging, which is the spiritual rationale behind Catherine's radical approach to material goods;   (2) Lady Poverty,   Catherine's   personification   of   this   spirit;   (3) kenosis, the scriptural word for the self-emptying of Christ.

I will treat other aspects of spiritual poverty when I come to the second line of the Mandate, "be poor."

Beggars For The Lord

The pilgrimage of Catherine is a pilgrimage into the mystery of poverty, which is really the mystery of the Poor Man, Christ. Christ became poor for love of us; he is especially found in the poor; pilgrims must become perfectly detached in order to travel and reach him.

She said once that if anyone writes her biography it should be called *By Poverty Possessed.* And she has asked that the cross on her grave be inscribed with the words, "She loved the poor." The very first word she received from the Lord about poverty was to give up all she possessed. Here is how she has articulated this word in our "Way of Life":

"Like all pilgrims the members travel in poverty to find security only in Christ." I like that. First I like the idea that we are pilgrims because that is what we are — Pilgrims of the Absolute.

Pilgrimage to me is a way of life because it is a totality of surrender. Such pilgrims whose life goal is the Absolute have no earthly abode. They have a place to live, a roof over their heads, but they are inwardly, always and totally, free and unattached, willing at a moment's notice to arise and go where the Lord and the Apostolate needs them.

A person whose way of life is pilgrimage does not take much on that pilgrimage, for in him the absence of the need to have becomes the need not to have. At first it may be that he really was indifferent to the few belongings that he took on his pilgrimage; but as he goes on, as his prayer deepens, he begins to experience and understand the passionate need not to have. It is one thing not to wish to possess, to be indifferent to possession, even to shed many possessions. But it is an entirely different experience to be shaken like a tree by a mighty wind with the desire not to have anything.

This passionate desire to be hollow, to be empty, as well as empty-handed, transforms poverty into that beautiful companion that Saint Francis always talked about. A heart once permeated with a passionate desire for total poverty — "not having" — begins to empty itself until it becomes a hollow for a naked Child to sleep in, until it becomes a tree for a Naked Man to die on.

At this point I approach the question of poverty in Madonna House on my knees, begging the Lord to give each of its present and future members the gift of this passionate desire "of the need not to have." Generosity will draw us all to total dispossession. I think Our Lady is praying quietly that, slowly but surely, all will divest themselves of all possessions.

A further aspect of poverty is intensely dear to my heart, and not only to mine: I am fully convinced that it is intensely dear to God's heart! With an unshakable faith I believe that the Lord has raised us to be beggars! Because the majority of the earth's inhabitants were beggars, someone had to enter that no-man's land that everyone seems to forget about — or to enter, not with their lives, but only through their money. Some Christians have to be beggars, that is, voluntary fools for Christ's sake.

I think God called us to this Apostolate to be such individual and collective beggars. As you know, we beg everything that we can, everywhere in our Apostolate. True, we do have to buy some goods, but we beg whenever possible and feasible. I hope that we will do this always until the parousia. In fact, I want to say directly and simply, that if we stop begging we shall disappear from the mind of God, even though we might seemingly be very successful on the face of the earth.   (WL)

Why do we actually, literally, give up everything? Because pilgrims of the Apostolate must depend absolutely on God. Pilgrims cannot be weighed down with many possessions. The interior emptiness created in the pilgrim's heart will then be a cradle for the Child, a bed for the Man of Sorrows. Such a practice of poverty is foolishness, but it is what we are called to live out. Most of the people in the world live with only the bare necessities of life. We are called by God to enter that no-man's land *actually*, and not just by prayer or financial assistance. It is *thus* we identify with the poor:

> We are beggars for the Lord. Alleluia! We are beggars for the Lord, first for the poor we serve everywhere, and secondly for ourselves.

This has been God's desire, his mandate to me when I first started way back in 1930 in the slums of Toronto. I knew well then and very clearly (as I know well now and very clearly) that we must remain beggars — poor men always. Even though some of us might earn a salary or be engaged in getting money through our Madonna House Mission Shop, nevertheless, beggars we shall remain, fundamentally and always, for it would be against the Spirit of Madonna House to stop begging, that spirit that has been given to me as a Foundress. (PTW, 29)

A few other quotations will show you how Catherine expands on the above themes:

I beg — we of the apostolate beg — because we are in love with a Beggar who is God. Love does such things; it cannot help itself. Those of us who fall in love with God — passionately, utterly — feel impelled by faith, reason, and love, to imitate him, to identify ourselves with him, to become one with him, to be poor like him, depending, in our day to day existence, on utter trust in our Beloved and his words. (SL #115, 1962)

Begging kills pride, teaches simplicity, makes faith grow, and love prosper. It also identifies us with all the poor beggars of the world who personally and collectively are Christ. When begging is done not only for oneself but for others, then the fear of hell recedes. One feeds and clothes and nurses and gives drink to the hungry, thirsty, imprisoned, the sick — not only out of one's bounty: We beg for thousands, and, as you know, thousands are fed with the goods of this world. But what is more, they are also fed spiritual food because we voluntarily and totally identified ourselves with them, and therefore brought God to them, crying the Gospel with our lives and bringing the hopeless hope. (SL #94, 1962)

Begging brings along with it a host of virtues. The first amongst them is humility, the fact that we are indeed poor before God, and all that we have is from him. In a small way, it brings to bear the ingenuity that the poor have to exercise to keep body and soul together. This is a very small way that we in our person and in our body realize how the poor feel, and this brings us closer to God's beloved ones, the really poor.   (SL #98, 1962)

One final reason for begging is what I call Catherine's "new economics of love." All her life she tried to get people to *share* their earthly goods. There is enough for all if we share:

Do you know what the song of poverty is? Sharing. Christ was given money by many, I imagine, since Judas kept a purse. Christ wanted to share everything all of the time. I visualize his poverty as sharing. Somehow I sense, and I dare to say that I know, that unless we begin to live the Gospel in its purity, we shall perish. To live the Gospel we must share.   (Pov)

Begging is a way of stimulating and creating a new economics in regards to material goods:

Another reason — and a most excellent one — is to give other people the opportunity to acquire great merit. For graces are poured on those who pour out their money or their time or their talents in acts of charity. If nobody begged, how many would give? If nobody gave, how much saddened the world would be — and how much more the God of Charity would grieve! Remember the words of St. Paul: "God loves a cheerful giver!" Maybe he loves a cheerful beggar too, for it is the beggar who creates the giver!   (SL #115, 1962)

In our day, if the new economics of love took hold, literally millions of people could be fed and clothed and supported. The food bank is a modern expression of this. Surplus food is taken to a main depot where it is distributed to those in need. This is exactly what our concept of begging accomplishes. People know that we do not simply beg for ourselves, but mostly for others. We take what we need, but most of what is given to us goes to others.

What is the mechanism behind all this? Love. Sharing. The surplus is there. People must be prompted to give. Then there must be people willing to donate their time and buildings and energy to distribute the goods. More charity. That's all it takes, really. And in our world today, this could be applied not only to goods of all kinds, but services as well. Could we not exchange services with one another — the barter system of the old days — instead of selling everything all the time? The new economics of love — this is what our begging seeks to foster.

During his life on earth Jesus lived both ways of poverty. During his time in Nazareth he worked and received payment and lived like everybody else. But when he left Nazareth and began his public ministry, he chose to stop working and depend totally upon his Father's providence for food, clothing, and housing. (It seems he didn't even always have the latter during his ministry: "The foxes have dens, the birds have their nests, but the Son of Man has nowhere to lay his head.") Catherine has been led by God to choose this latter way for the reasons given above. Jesus said that a laborer is worthy of his hire, and that if you try to live and share the Gospel with others, you may depend on the Father to take care of you. St. Paul acknowledges the legitimacy of this way (1 Cor 9:14).

Catherine knows very well all the sophisticated reasons why in today's world one should not beg: there are enough

poor already; "Why don't you work for a living like every
one else?"; begging is demeaning for the human person; it
pulls the rug out from under one's dignity as a self-
supporting, self-sufficient human being, etc.

We know all these reasons — and we struggle with
them. But begging is not a rational, sophisticated approach
to material support. It is a foolish, Gospel way of faith, and it
requires faith to understand and live it. It is meant to be a
sign of the kingdom, a living proof of the providence of the
Father of Jesus. It is not that we are not working! But our
chief work (as the Lord said) is to *believe*, to *live* the Gospel. If
we are trying to live the Gospel, trying to share the truth and
love of the Gospel with others, then Jesus said we could
depend on his Father. This is the way Catherine chose,
guided by the Spirit.

A Way To The Poor Man

Catherine has written and spoken about poverty
perhaps even more than about love. Poverty, for her, however, is much more than one of the virtues. She
writes: "Poverty is not only a virtue to practice. Poverty is
also a state, a way of life."   (SL #148, 1963)

Fedotov (*The Russian Religious Mind*) in writing about
St. Theodosius, the saint who became the prototype for all
subsequent Russian sanctity, says: "Poverty, humility, and
love . . . with Theodosius are not ascetic means for shaping
Christian personality. They are rather an end in themselves,
expressing different sides of the same personality: the incarnate Christ . . ."   (129)

Because of sin and our disorientation from God we have acquired an enormous amount of interior and exterior baggage. Poverty is not the form which love must take: it is the opposite side of all real loving. There can be no real love without the stripping, the getting rid of, the emptying (kenosis) of the false accruements of sin which "cling so easily." If we desire to trust God more, we must let go of false self-assurance. If we wish to love others more, we must let go of our selfish ways. And so on with all the other movements of love. Each movement has a reverse "poverty" dimension, and so the pilgrimage to Christ takes the form of love/poverty.

Someone asked once why love is not mentioned in this first paragraph of the Mandate if it's the most important virtue. The *essence of love in our present condition* is described there: Love is the journey to meet Christ in the poor through a complete stripping of the self.

Why is Catherine "by poverty possessed"? Why does her spirituality take on this particular coloration? The ultimate answer is lost in the mystery and election of God, how he wishes to attract people with his grace. But her *life* affords some explanations as to how this grace was communicated and nurtured.

The Russian spiritual tradition is very strong on seeing Christ in the poor and being awed by his *kenosis*, his identification with us. This same Theodosius, as a young man, used to go into the fields and work with the peasants. His mother was scandalized. He simply answered:

> Listen, Mother, I implore. Our Lord and God Jesus Christ, became poor and humiliated himself, giving us the example that we also should humiliate ourselves for his sake.

Catherine saw her parents themselves go to serve Christ in the poor when beggars came to the door of their home.

Her mother, as was mentioned, used to go to serve the poor. Catherine often went along:

> I always knew about the poor, as my mother had taught me so well about poverty. I remember my youth when my mother would say, "Well, Catherine, let's get this knapsack together. I'm going to fill it with what is needed for the safe deliverance of so and so's baby." Mother did a bit of nursing, especially in regards to midwifery. And so we walked ten miles. The knapsack was heavy. She would say, "No, it's no heavier than the Cross that Christ carried. You think about that cross, and you think about poverty, because Christ was very poor. In fact he was totally poor for you. He died naked on the cross." (Pov)

St. Francis of Assisi is one of Catherine's greatest loves and inspirations among the saints — perhaps the greatest. Their love affair began when she was a child going to school in Egypt. Francis was another powerful vehicle for the communication of the grace of poverty. She describes it in terms of a fragmentary scene from her childhood:

> I was a very small child in kindergarten. Egypt, palms, a nun belonging to the Order of Our Lady of Zion, and a big school at Ramleh, which was what you would call a suburb of Alexandria. The statue of St. Francis in some kind of shrine, surrounded by bouganville or some vivid red flowers. This is how it comes to me. And the little young Sister with rosy cheeks in a white religious garb, surrounded by us kindergarten kids, telling us the story of St. Francis, and my running out and clapping my hands at St. Francis saying, "I will be like you. I will go and be very poor and the birds will eat out of my hands, and if anybody gives me bread, I will share it with the first poor child that I ever see on the road." The picture fades.   (HMCB)

The circumstances of Catherine's life were also power-ful media for the grace of poverty. Born into a fairly wealthy family, she lost literally everything due to the revolution. At the point of starvation in Finland, she promised God that if he allowed her to live she would give him her life. She did live and came to the "new world." Though starting at the bottom of the social ladder as all immigrants do, she eventu-ally became fairly well off again. This experience of wealth/poverty/wealth made her ask the radical question: "What does it all really mean?"

She often opened the Scriptures for a passage, and she invariably opened to Matthew 19:21, "If you would be perfect, go and sell all you possess and give it to the poor, and you will have treasure in heaven, and come and follow me." This was the text the great St. Anthony heard, the text St. Francis heard, and so many others down through the ages.

Fedotov says that the Russians do not think so much of imitating Christ as following him. Perhaps "imitate" is too abstract for the Russian incarnational mind. "Follow him," "Do what he did," makes more sense. In the following pas-sage Catherine had arrived at the point in her life where a radical decision is being asked of her. Several threads of her life came together: To follow Christ one must begin where he began, in Bethlehem; Bethlehem was a cave; the cave today is with the poor in the slums; Christ is there. The vision of St. Francis and his total dispossession returns:

> I was praying about the deep, deep sense of these words, these strange, haunting words, "Follow me . . . going to the poor . . . being poor . . . being one with them . . . one with Me." Perhaps I was asking God to give me a clear answer, but he very seldom does, because he demands faith. But his mercy is so great that occasionally shafts of light came through. I thought to myself: "OK, if I

have to go back to the state of poverty in which I was when I first landed on this North American continent, then it means that I have to live the way I lived then. I have only one alternative — to start at Bethlehem and allow this vocation to be born there."

Now, what was Bethlehem in the context of this travail of my soul? It meant a cave . . . it meant the slums, plain and simple . . . to become one with the poor, and hence with Christ, by living exactly like them. The little girl who clapped her hands before St. Francis and wanted to be poor like him . . .   (HMCB)

I think at this juncture of her spiritual life was born her deep understanding of the "following of Christ." For her, it is not simply carrying one's cross. It is attempting, both inwardly and outwardly, to take the same journey in our world, out of love for Jesus, that Jesus took out of love for us. Thus, as she ponders how to begin her following of Christ, she asks the question, "How did Jesus begin, and where?" He began in a cave, amidst the poor. "Where is the poorest spot in my environment?" In the slums. "Right. That's where I must go."

The following of Christ is the inner identification with the mysteries of his life. Then, because of her deep incarnationalism, Catherine sought to actually *live as Christ lived*. Bethlehem, Nazareth, the Public Life, living on the providence of God, Golgotha, Resurrection — she not only seeks inner participation in these mysteries but seeks to incarnate them in a life-style in keeping with the actual life of Christ.

Thus, Catherine's deepest insights about poverty concern her following of the Poor Christ — not acquiring the "virtue" of poverty, not simply being poor as a "witness" or fostering "sharing." These too. But primarily what drives her is a desire to identify with her Beloved who was rich and became poor for love of her.

On a Final Promises Day here one year, Catherine, in a poem, contrasted the lovely surroundings of Madonna House with the poor circumstances of her own Final Promises Day in the slums. It is one of her (and our) favorite poems. The concluding lines reveal that her Beloved is above all the Poor One:

> The room became immense, and a thousand voices sang my wedding to the King. I know his Mother was there, whose name I bear. The rest I could not see, blinded as I was with ecstasy.
>
> Yes, I would not exchange my wedding day to God, in that gray, shabby room, on that gray October day, for any other day anywhere!
>
> I praise his name. My heart sings gratitude, even as angels sing before his throne unceasingly. For behold, the Pauper who wedded me in the slums, in a dilapidated house, a shabby room, was a great King, Christ the Lord, and I became that day a queen, his spouse.
>
> Alleluia! Alleluia! Alleluia! (JI, 1)

And to the community she writes:

> Being the bride of a Poor Man, the Pauper, who during his public life had nowhere to lay his head and died naked on the cross, one wonders why even a shadow of a temptation should penetrate into the mind of any staff worker against this holy, joyous poverty. (SL #69, 1961)

Besides seeing the goal of the journey as a wedding with the Pauper Christ, Catherine interprets the whole life of the Lord in terms of poverty. We have already touched upon

Bethlehem and Nazareth. The *leaving* of Nazareth was poverty:

> It must have been tremendously difficult for him to leave his mother, even if he knew that some relatives would take care of her; he loved her deeply and profoundly, it must have been a tremendous act of poverty. He really gave all he possessed. (Pov)

His *allowing himself to be tempted* was poverty:

> He allowed himself to be tempted by the devil. Stop for a moment and think: God allowing himself to be tempted by the devil! Incredible! His human poverty glowed like a thousand diamonds . . . in that act of allowing himself to become truly human — letting himself be tempted. (Pov)

She mentions his poverty of not having a place to sleep; the total dependence on his Father for food and clothing; the poverty of his rejection and loneliness. In all this she seeks to follow him:

> Many days I come to my desk, and it seems to me that I am the one who is following Christ, step by step, across his three years, across his miracles, across his rejection by so many, and in that very rejection I see the abyss of poverty. The poverty of Christ is before us. What are we going to do about it? (Pov)

Lady Poverty

In the first chapter of Catherine's book on poverty (which I have just quoted) she spoke of it as a virtue. The second chapter begins:

Yes in the first chapter I explained how I fell in love with poverty. But I did not know, I never dreamed that poverty would take over.

She would appear somewhere in the corner of my heart. There she was, just as I dreamt she might have been. I would say she is kind and gentle, and she whispered softly also little ideas about my giving up this, and my giving up that. (Pov)

Then, throughout perhaps a third of the manuscript, she speaks of *Lady Poverty*.

No doubt the name "Lady Poverty" comes from St. Francis, though the core imagery for Catherine is different. "Yes, poverty just won't let me be. I remembered St. Francis who used to call poverty his Lady Fair. But to me poverty is more like a sister, a twin sister, who walks where I walk, eats where I eat, sleeps where I sleep." St. Francis loved Poverty as a medieval knight loved and served his Lady Fair. Catherine says that she thinks of her more as a *sister*. But it is more profound than that. I wish to share with you some remarkable texts concerning this personification of poverty; then I have some interpretations of my own.

Toward the end of her life Catherine gave the following interpretation of how Lady Poverty was born. It is extremely beautiful and rich in meaning. The first "she" in this passage is Mary:

> She watched. And then she stood under his cross. Blood dripped from his wounds, for he had been flagellated before he was crucified. She probably could hear each drop fall. Poverty was by her side. Poverty knew that very soon she and Mary would be one. And so it was.
>
> He died. They took him from the cross and laid him naked upon her lap. Yes, naked he came from her womb,

and naked he was laid on her knees. The Romans and Jews did not pay attention to nakedness the way we do. She held him with her two hands, and at that moment two poverties met — Christ leaving Mary, and Mary offering Christ to the Father. Did they blend? Did Poverty feel that she had reached the apex of her life, the summit of all things that she could ever think about?

I think she did. I think this was the moment she could really be called Lady Poverty of the shimmering garment which St. Francis dressed her with. She must have lifted her arms and covered her face with them, because what she saw was so mysterious, so profound, so immense, that it allowed her to have within her heart the meeting of two poverties. It was very strange, because it was really one poverty; and yet it was two — the poverty of his going, and the poverty of his coming.

He left her (Lady Poverty) to proclaim his love to the world. He came to her to proclaim his love to the world. He came to her because now anyone could touch love in his very body.   (Pov)

Isn't this a profoundly moving passage? Out of the two deepest poverties the world has ever known — Mary's loss of her son and Jesus laying down his life — Lady Poverty is born.

Now, in traditional theology, who is poured forth upon the world at this moment? The Holy Spirit. I believe that for Catherine, Lady Poverty is a personification of the Holy Spirit. Catherine comes close to saying this herself:

I listen to Lady Poverty very carefully, for, in a sense, she is the voice of God. You must therefore listen to her, for God valued her so very much. She is not only your love, but she is the love of God.   (Pov)

When we come to the line, "Listen to the Spirit, He will lead you," we shall see that, for Catherine, the Spirit is primarily he who explains to us the words of Christ, as Jesus said he would. We might say that as the Spirit teaches us about love, so also the Spirit (Lady Poverty) teaches us about poverty, which, as I said, is now the necessary component of all loving. Not everything Catherine has said about Lady Poverty fits in perfectly with this interpretation, but I believe it's the one which best accounts for how Lady Poverty personally *functions in her life*. (It may also be akin to the Russian *Sophia*, to which it has many similarities.)

However, this Lady Poverty is a very mysterious Lady! Just as poverty is not simply one of the virtues for Catherine, but a way equal to love, so to say that Lady Poverty is simply the virtue of poverty personified would be a very minimal view. She does say that Lady Poverty is the "humblest of all the virtues" (68), but then, in what may be her last word on the nature of Lady Poverty, she has this to say:

> I saw Lady Poverty bedecked in beautiful garments. She was sitting at the right hand of the Lord. There was joy on her countenance, and gladness, that he was dying. She turned towards me and she said, "Catherine, you see me here with the Lord. That is because of my tremendous love for him." She beckoned, and from somewhere, Love came and sat by her side; hope came from the other side. The Lord smiled and said, "Hope, love, and faith is what you are made of, my dear friend, Lady Poverty.
>
> "Now, kneel down!" They all knelt down, but especially Lady Poverty, who put her face in his lap. He put his hand over her head and smiled as he did so. He said: "Go forth! Faith, Hope and Love will be with you, but what you must do is change the hearts of men. I will give you one word to take wherever you go amongst them . . . The words is 'share.' Tell them if they do not share their possessions, I will take them away." (Pov)

These are the closing words of the manuscript.

Here Lady Poverty clearly is not the Holy Spirit, but on the other hand, she is made up of the three greatest virtues. Whatever her nature (multiple, no doubt) in Catherine's mind, she is an exalted symbol. I like her as a personification of the Spirit because Catherine often says we should fall in love with her, and how can you fall in love with a virtue? "Lady Poverty — the beautiful one whom we should desire above all things, because she is God's Beloved!" (WLIGI 52) She also is to be sought within: ". . . she is not easy to find. We have to make a pilgrimage to find her, and that pilgrimage is within ourselves."   (Pov)

Whatever her nature, it is she who conducts us through the mysteries of the Poor Man:

> Do I wish to take the hand of the Lady Poverty and go to see the Christ Child born? Am I ready to go with Lady Poverty to Golgotha and beyond? If I am ready to be crucified in nakedness on the other side of the cross, with Lady Poverty smiling at me from below, then I shall possess the kingdom of God. But above all, I shall possess him, and by his grace and her help, I can give him to others.   (Pov)

> If we should fall in love with her, how simple and glorious our lives would become.   (WLIGI)

Kenosis

Another dimension of the mystery of the Poor Christ is described by the Greek word "kenosis" (empty) and comes from St. Paul's letter to the Philippians (2:6-8):

Though he was in the form of God, he did not deem equality with God something to be grasped at. Rather, he emptied himself and took the form of a slave. Being born in the likeness of man he was known to be of human estate, and it was thus that he humbled himself, obediently accepting even death, death on a cross.

This mystery of the kenosis of Christ is another way in which Catherine expresses the essence of poverty: "The kenosis we must undergo, the emptying of self so as to be filled with Christ." (SL #109)

As far as possible, Christ stripped himself of his divine prerogatives for love of us. The circumstances of his birth, his hidden life in Nazareth, his suffering of rejection and misunderstanding, and finally, even allowing himself to experience an abandonment by the Father — such were the earthly forms of his kenosis.

The journey inward is thus a journey into the mystery of kenosis where we are purified of fear, human respect, anxieties, the distortions of the mind, etc. It is a kind of death which we can undergo only because of Christ's own kenosis: "We meet, Beloved! Your descent is my ascent." ("Last Days of Advent," JI, I).

Fedotov says that "kenoticism is the most original creation of the Russian religious spirit." And Evdokimov states (*Le Christ Dans La Pensee Russe*): "The religious ideal of a people is formed partly from its very personal vision of God, partly from the artistic, iconographic image it forms of Christ. There is a Flemish Christ, a Spanish Christ, a Greek Christ. There is also a Russian Christ who exhibits the essential gospel characteristic of kenosis — of the humble Brother, of the humiliated, of he who is always with the poor, the sick, the suffering" (41).

The Russians, at the dawn of their evangelization,

could read the Gospel in their own language. And from the very beginning they were awed by the self-humiliation of God. Catherine writes:

> Kenosis, you might say, is the basic core idea of Russian spirituality. For the poustinik, the most powerful of all his thoughts and prayers should be to empty himself as Christ emptied himself by his Incarnation.   (P, 139)

> Why enter into this kenosis? "In order," says St. Paul, "to make up for what is wanting in the sufferings of Christ on behalf of his body, which is the Church." In order to share in the sufferings of Christ. This is the whole aim and goal of kenosis. This is where it leads.   (P, 143)

As far as I know, Catherine never uses the Greek word opposite to kenosis which is plerosis (fullness), but she very often does speak of this fullness: self-emptying is only so as to be *filled* with Christ; that he might achieve his *full stature* in us; that we might be *filled* with light, etc.

With our prideful, sinful eyes, when we look upon Christ living in Nazareth, washing the disciples' feet, and dying on the cross, we name these actions "self-emptying." For *us* they would be self-emptying. Positively, we can say that this is how divine life acts when in our world. In Christ, kenosis and plerosis are one and the same. We, as sinners, need to first empty ourselves so that the divine life can manifest itself in us. "He (the poustinik) has become so empty that he is simply one who carries God" (P, 134). Catherine's is certainly a "kenosis Christology," an ever-deepening identification with Christ the Humble One so as to manifest the divine life in the world.

CHAPTER FOUR

The Cross

* * *

Take up My cross
(their cross)
— being one with them
— one with Me.

So we are on a journey into the heart of the Trinity, into
the home of Nazareth, into the womb of the Church, into
the heart of Mary, guided by faith and the spirit of the
beatitudes. We are pilgrimaging at every moment, driven on
by the nostalgia for paradise, drawn by the love of the Great
Pilgrim, Christ. It is an exciting, restless adventure into the
poor, into the mystery of Lady Poverty, following Christ into
the depths of his kenosis.

Kenosis and poverty are almost identical in Catherine's
mind: because of sin, we have made ourselves rich in the
wrong way. Jesus, who was God — full of the richness of the
divine life — came and made himself poor for our sakes. He
did not lose, of course, anything pertaining to his divinity;
nor was his coming "beneath his dignity." Rather, by hum-
bling himself and hiding his divinity among us, he revealed
another dimension of the divine love.

In this chapter we are concerned with three final themes at the heart of the Mandate: the cross, identification, and the ongoing passion of Christ in his Body on earth.

The Cross

The way of self-emptying, of kenosis, of poverty, is necessarily *painful* because of the condition in which we find ourselves. Hence, the cross is an essential characteristic of the pilgrim's journey. Also, the theme of identification (with others and especially with Christ) means that we are not alone in our sufferings. One of the most painful aspects of suffering is that it tends to isolate us. We say "misery loves company." Company helps us to carry our misery. It is much easier to suffer something with others than to suffer alone. So, identification means that there is *solidarity in our suffering*. Our cross is the cross of Jesus and of others. We are not on a lonely walk.

Many events of Catherine's life brought home to her the lesson that suffering was unavoidable, and that to embrace it was the height of wisdom. She was driven from her native land; almost starved to death in Finland; became a refugee in a strange land; went through the break-up of her apostolate at least twice (in Toronto and Harlem). After she came up to Combermere in 1947, in a letter to Fr. Furfey her spiritual director, she reflected upon this lesson of the cross she was being taught:

> The way of the night became something familiar. Yet I did not see quite the why and the wherefore of it all, but now I see. And if God grants me a certain length of days, I want to write my third and last book. It is there, already in my mind and heart. It has to come out, for somehow or other I think it holds an answer to the problem of the Lay

Apostolate. Its content, rather simple. The theme is worn, threadbare, and as old as Christianity itself. The only new thing is the accent of its rediscovery by the individual. The tumbleweed of God that I seem to be can only do that: Give the old theme a personalized accent.

The ideas are old: to die to self, to follow the naked Christ; and charity as the only real foundation of all works of God. Detachment, utter, absolute poverty of spirit. Trite words, yet burning like a fire within my heart. Because I think I touched, at this late hour, the very essence, their heart. I see it all now. I see the apostolate at the foot of Golgotha, see the need for hearts so burning with love that, firmly and simply, they will ascend *the Hill*, and having reached the summit look at themselves. With calm, strong hands they will remove all shreds of any garments that may yet cling to them. With a love unknown to them they will move the hearts of men beyond any words or deeds done in the past. They will lay down with arms outstretched on the cross that has awaited their voluntary coming since the dawn of days.

Lie there they must, of their own free will, without fear, without haste. Lie down for no other reason than that their love for God is so great that alone this cruciform death will assuage its burning wounds, its incredible, ever-consuming hunger. The feel of nails being driven in will then become for them the song of songs: "My Beloved to me and I to him." It will be the end of the greatest loneliness the souls of men know. It will be the final gift of the apostle to the apostolate, the gift supreme that will produce undreamed of results. For they will be God's results, born in utter surrender and love of his creature.

That is the soul of the apostolate, that death to self. Oh, Father, how tragic it is that it took me years to get here! How silly that I did not see that so little mattered except that inner path. I have always loved God, always known that love is pain and sacrifice. But Combermere showed me that love is death, and death is life. Old words repeated *ad nauseam* in spiritual writings. Words, read and re-read and re-read — commented on, even by me, in the pride of foolish, human wisdom. I thought I knew what they meant. But the *Journey Inward* has been long; the end is not far.

Only now do I understand and see. It took the last convention * to batter down that silly pride of mine. It took its blows to crush me to the earth. It took its sharp cutting to make me bleed, and bleeding see that wounds are but part of the surrender. I had to be slapped around to come to my senses. Amen! Alleluia! God be blessed for the pain of last January, and for the bitterness it brought me. Alleluia!

For now I am free. The last detachment is a thing of the past. Before God, I am detached from Friendship House. In the right sense, I mean. Detached from the desire and the shadow of authority and power, of motherhood and of all the rights of a foundress and what have you. I know now what will help Friendship House and what I must give it. I must lift it up, wrap it up, along with the gift I have to give him whom I loved so long and so much and so imperfectly. I have to walk up the Holy Hill. I have to, finally and completely, strip myself and lay down on that Cross he had prepared for me from the dawn of days. Only then will my restless soul be at peace. Only then will the tumbleweed of God find a mooring place. To die to self so that Friendship House may live. To die to self so that God may live in me utterly, completely. That is the end of this Journey Inward. That is the only answer that will make the lay apostolate secure and firm. That is the theme of the book that I must write. Pray for me.   (FL)

---

* The Friendship House Convention in Chicago where most of the members voted to take a direction different from what Catherine believed was her original spirit.

This extraordinary passage contains the heart of her teachings about the cross: the following of Christ demands the absolute stripping of self, a becoming naked with the crucified Christ on the Cross. This is the source of all real fruitfulness in the kingdom.

Before Catherine left Harlem she wrote a series of articles for *Friendship House News* entitled: "It All Goes Together." They were meditations on the nature of the Lay Apostolate. She chose one of these articles for the first issue of her Madonna House, Combermere, newspaper, RESTORATION. After describing the various stages of the life of Christ which the lay apostle must traverse, she wrote:

> And now the Pasch, Gethsemane, Holy Thursday, Herod, Pilate, the Way of the Cross . . . on fire with love of God the lay apostle will faithfully follow Christ to the end. He must, for unless he does his apostolate will be but a pious dream without substance — a humanitarian endeavor that cannot be lifted up to the Man of Sorrows. No, it is all or nothing. A true lay apostle will take the path to the Holy Hill. This Journey Inward, this school of love will lead to death to self, and to a resurrection in love. (Dec., 1947)

And in her instruction to the community over the years, the necessity and centrality of the cross is a constant theme:

> I have been thinking much lately about the spirit of the Institute and what its outstanding features are. We all know that the Spirit of our Institute is expressed in the cross we wear, with the words 'pax-caritas' inscribed on it. It is not easy to reach that cross, this immense cross of Christ, to lay on it and be stretched unto infinity in charity. To arrive at this immense stretching out presupposes fidelity and perseverance, and a growth of vision within

the members of the Institute. Wounded and tired, exhausted even, they must drag themselves painfully up to the skull of the hill, their bruised knees and elbows moving inch by inch along the ground towards that desired goal, the cross.

Without fidelity, without perseverance, without the growing vision, they might not reach the cross. They might give in to tiredness and exhaustion and to the darkness of the night. There will come a time then of stretching, to fulfill the first word written on this beautiful cross of ours — caritas. Yes, then will come the stretching.

What is needed for that stretching, what weapons, what tools of the Spirit? What are needed are human beings who empty themselves so as to be filled with the immense Christ. Christ alone fills completely his immense cross. It is obvious that we will not be able to be crucified on his cross unless we are close to his side. Stop and think for a moment of the immense gift that God has given us by his Incarnation. To be one with him. To be sharers of his divine life. To be one in love. To die in this way requires knowledge, prayer, generosity, courage, which men will call foolhardy. They will call it stupidity. In a word, it will require us to become fools for Christ's sake. For the foolishness of the saints is wisdom before the face of God.   (SL #9, 1957)

Where can we go where there is no cross? How foolish, pitiful, our attempts to escape, when once knowing the will of God for us in our vocation we try to run away from it. And all we do is add to the cross that God has given to each of us. Our own cross of frustration, guilt, and a thousand other things will slowly, like weeds, clutter up our lives. We are deciding, then, to live a life according to our own rules, not his. The temptation to descend from the cross of God's choosing, to leave him alone there to escape the pain — that is natural. But we are Christians.

We have a supernatural destiny. So think of Christ on the cross when temptation comes. Think of Gethsemane. What would have happened to you and me if he had given in to the temptation of Gethsemane and not gone on to crucifixion? An impossible thought you say; and yet, one that comes to mind!   (SL #88, 1961)

I cannot visualize a love story with God without a cross. To me the cross is *the thing*. I desire it, I accept it. I ask for the grace never to fear it, because, at the end, I shall finally know its joy.

Of course the cross is there. When I talked about the cross I think you misunderstood what I meant. For me the cross is the key to him whom my heart loves. Without the cross there is no Easter. Unless I die on the cross I cannot see him in heaven. I must lie on the cross that he made for me. It is certainly not the one I am making for myself.

God embraced the cross for us because he wanted to. For this he was born. For this we are born also: To lie on it with him. I mean these words literally, but I think you don't understand me, and that is the problem. Think of your vocation as the glory of the cross, what he has done for us.   (SL #104, 1962)

We have a transcript of a talk given by Catherine in 1956. We call it "The Spirit of Madonna House Apostolate." We consider it to be one of the best descriptions Catherine ever gave of our way of life. In it she said:

You have heard the plan of God outlined for you. The miracle of that plan is that God invites you and me to participate in it. To put it perhaps a bit more simply, the plan is this: Behold the crucifixion! A simple cross and a Man upon it who thirsts: "*Sitio*." Does he thirst for water, for wine? Maybe. But he thirsts primarily for souls. Our vocation is so utterly simple that it is impossible to describe it.

It is to burn, to do the will of God in the duty of the moment. To die to self. To live in obedience, poverty, love, and chastity. To live in the present moment. To have no one who belongs to you, and you belonging to no one but God. To be ready to be crucified, in the mystical sense, on the cross of the will of God. To be ready to be crucified by men. You will be.

"He was obedient unto death." Crosses are not fashionable in the 20th century. It is simply death, but, oh, how profound! How strange and mysterious. It is a death which carries within itself the very seeds of life. It is the simple, profound, complete death to self which opens all doors.

When the "I" has been completely surrendered then the hallways of the Kingdom of Heaven have opened upon the earth. Greater love has no man than to die for his fellow man. Our vocation is to die that we may live and give life to others. To the extent that I die, to that extent my neighbor lives, to that extent I bring the light of Christ.   (SL #140, 1963)

It is an old message; nothing new here. "Take up your cross every day and follow Me." There is no other way to be united with Christ. Because of sin, because of the condition of the world, pain is unavoidable. The cross is the painful part of poverty, which is inseparable from loving. The cross is not fashionable today. There are many currents in spirituality and psychology seeking a way around the cross, seeking some way "out of it." The only way out is to lie on it. One of the most authentic aspects of Catherine's spirituality is this absolute necessity and centrality of the cross. As we go through the Mandate you will see it connected with every attempt at real loving. She sees her vocation as leading people to Golgotha so they can learn there how to love:

I know one thing — I cannot rest. I see the pain of Christ so vividly, I see the tears of Christ so clearly. I hear always the cry of Christ. Sleeping or waking, it seems in my ears I hear the word, "*Sitio*," "I thirst." And then I see Christ waiting, waiting, waiting, a Beggar for our hearts. He is a waiting Beggar, a waiting Pauper at the crossroads of the endless everywheres of the earth.

It seems to me that I am a runner, called by God to bring souls to Golgotha. They are young, loving souls, on a journey of his most Holy Will. I have to teach them a little bit how to love him. But my real job is to bring them to Golgotha at twelve-thirty on Good Friday. And to me, every day is Good Friday. I let them look at him, dying there for love of them. Then I let him teach them how to love.   (SL #56, 1960)

Now, simply embracing pain and suffering for their own sake is not life-giving. Suffering and pain in themselves are not goods to be embraced. It is not a matter of desiring suffering in some masochistic sense. For Christians, the cross is always a matter of embracing *someone* — either ourselves, another person, or Christ. The deepest aspect of the mystery we are now going to enter is this: true Christian love is the simultaneous embracing of Christ, self, and others. For a person with faith in Christ, we are never simply embracing a bloody cross with no one on it. Our hearts embrace the feet of our Beloved, and the hurting members of ourselves and others. This is the mystery we would like to investigate now.

"I WOULD LIKE TO BRING TO THE FAMILY THAT GOD HAS DEIGNED TO ESTABLISH THROUGH ME THE VERY ESSENCE OF MY SPIRITUALITY. . . THE TRINITY. . ."

(Russian icon: Rublev's Trinity)

"IT IS THERE, IN THE MYSTERY OF THE EUCHARIST, THAT WE GET THE STRENGTH TO LIVE THE LAW OF LOVE."

(Catherine receiving Communion from Fr. Paul, in the island chapel at Madonna House)

"THE SPIRIT OF MADONNA HOUSE IS ONE OF ARDENT ZEAL FOR THE GLORY OF GOD, THE SALVATION OF SOULS, AND THE RESTORATION OF ALL THINGS TO CHRIST THROUGH MARY." *(Our Lady of Combermere)*

"MADONNA HOUSE SPIRIT IS THAT OF A FAMILY . . . THE FAMILY OF NAZARETH . . . WHICH WAS 'A COMMUNITY OF PERFECT CHARITY AND LOVE'."
(Class of Applicants on a tour of some of the roots of the Apostolate, with three of the staff)

"OUR JOURNEY OF LIFE . . . SHOULD BE A JOURNEY INWARD, TO MEET THE GOD WHO DWELLS WITHIN US." *(Inside of one of the Madonna House poustinias)*

"SIMPLICITY. . . WHAT IS MORE SIMPLE THAN THE LIFE OF A CARPENTER IN THE MIDST OF A SMALL VILLAGE?" *(Jim building a wall for the Marian Meadows chapel)*

"FOR US, THE WILL OF THE FATHER IS REVEALED BY THE NEEDS OF THE APOSTOLATE AT EVERY GIVEN MOMENT OF OUR DAY." *(Mary tanning sheepskins)*

"WE ARE ENGANGED IN AN ORDINARY LIFE, SEEMINGLY SIMPLE, UNADVENTUROUS, MONOTONOUS, A LIFE OF DAILY TASKS DONE WITH GREAT LOVE FOR GOD AND NEIGH-BOR." *(Alma teaching Dina the intricacies of the herb garden)*

"TRUST BELONGS TO THOSE WHO HAVE THE HEART OF A CHILD."
(Nancy watching a small child while his parents visit)

"CELEBRATION IS A RETURN TO CHILDHOOD. IT IS SIMPLY THE ABILITY TO BEGIN TO WONDER AGAIN. IT TAKES THE EYES OF A CHILD TO SEE THAT, AND IT TAKES THE EYES OF A CHILD TO WONDER AND TO FEEL WITHIN HIS SOUL THE MUSIC OF CELEBRATION."
(Archbishop Raya (center) *celebrating his anniversary)*

"ARISE - GO! . . . .FAITH IS A PILGRIMAGE TOWARD THE ABSOLUTE. FAITH GIVES EVERY CHRISTIAN SANDALS AND A PILGRIM'S STAFF AND BIDS HIM TO ARISE AND GO IN SEARCH OF HIM WHOM EVERY CHRISTIAN LONGS FOR - GOD."

(Bridge connecting Catherine's island cabin, St. Kate's, to the mainland.)

"SIMPLICITY IS THE FRUIT OF LOVE. I SEE A PRIEST SITTING IN THE MIDST OF OTHER PEOPLE, JUST SITTING AND TALKING, TELLING THE MARVELS OF GOD. . . IT IS THE SIMPLICITY, THAT AUTHENTICITY, THAT SOMETHING THAT COMES FROM THE HEART AND NOT FROM A BOOK, THAT I WOULD ESPECIALLY LIKE THE REVEREND CLERGY TO GIVE US." *(Fr. Duffy (center) with two of the men in the pre-seminary program)*

"THE ORDINARINESS OF OUR DAYS IN MADONNA HOUSE, THE SIMPLICITY OF IT, THE HOSPITALITY OF IT — THAT IS THE ESSENCE OF MADONNA HOUSE."
(A. *Larry checking the year's cabbage crop, and B. Bill* (foreground) *and Bryan fix a car*)

DOROTHY DAY SAID OF CATHERINE THAT "SHE HAS THE GIFT OF A GREAT AND JOYOUS FAITH AND OF MAKING LIFE AN ADVENTURE, A PILGRIMAGE."

(*Catherine in front of Madonna House in Combermere*)

CHAPTER FIVE

Identification
With Christ In Pain

* * *

The first step of the journey into pain's transformation is described by Catherine in a wonderful mythological story entitled, "How Lady Pain Became So Beautiful."

From the dawn of time Lady Pain was Queen of an immense domain. "Few escaped her. At one time or another, in every man's life, she would come and visit him. She would bend down and, taking the person in her arms, hold him tight. When he was quite dead she would let him go" (NWP, 185). It wasn't until she met Christ on the cross that her nature was radically changed:

> She looked up and saw that he was dead. Slowly she walked away. She sat down by the side of a lake to rest. She saw her face reflected on the calm surface of the water. She did not like to see herself most of the time. But — what was this! Somehow her eyes had been purified and she saw beyond her ugliness to her beauty within.
>
> And that is why, ever since, men who are able to see more deeply know that Love wedded himself to Lady

Pain, and that Love can make her beautiful — as beautiful as she saw herself on that day of Love's death. (NWP, 185)

This is a very accurate account, in symbolic terms, of how pain begins to be transformed: by meeting Love on the Cross. To the eyes of faith, Christ is present in all pain, because he has come and suffered all our pains. For us, the universe is personal, and every one of our acts is ultimately joined to a Person — if we have faith. Further, our cross is also the cross of the poor, that is, every person. There is a solidarity in suffering. The only way we can fruitfully complete our pilgrimage is to carry our own cross, which is the cross of one another, which is the Cross of Christ.

A sky aflame is pale before a soul in love with God. The pain of all mankind is but a scratch before the pain of Christ's love. To burn, to love, to share the pain. That is my life, my only song, and its refrain.   (JI, II)

To share the pain, the pain of all mankind, which is Christ's pain. This is Catherine's life, her song.

There are basically two aspects of Catherine's understanding of identification, and both flow profoundly from the mystery of the Incarnation. The eternal Son of God really became Man, that is, identified himself with us as much as it was possible for him to do so. It was precisely by this identification that he saved us. His divine Personality entered into every area of our beings, and so rescued them from futility and death. His life, therefore, must penetrate every human person. It is the sublime vocation of the Christian to participate with Christ in the mystery of his continuing identification with the human race.

There are two movements:

(1) Christ identifies himself with each person;
(2) we are instruments of his Presence by our identification with others.

It is not a matter of losing our identity. Rather, we discover our identity by emptying ourselves of selfishness so that we truly can empathize and be compassionate toward every human being. The following poem/meditation expresses one of the graces propelling Catherine on her pilgrimage. It is the grace "To Be Everyone," which is the title she gave this reflection:

What am I? And who am I? One who dies a thousand · deaths yet stays alive. One who hangs upon a cross not made of wood, but of days and nights that merge and dance their endless dance of pain and delight.

One who walks in silence like a shroud, yet speaks for those who cannot speak, in an endless sea of words that storms, pleads, and batters away at hearts of stone that send my words back to me, fiery wounding darts of painful ecstasy.

One who is torn apart by all the pain of the ones who hunger and who thirst, whose shelter is the dusty streets of tropics, or the searing white wastes of snowy deserts.

I am the millions who seek him — and yet I found him. How can that be? Why must I live as if I were all others? It seems to me that I am torn apart, and that each piece of me is someone else in search of him whom I possess. And I must go, walk to my God, for he is the Way, which means I walk upon Love itself.

Note that he walks that way still. But how can one walk on feet that are nailed and hands made fast to beam and cross?

The mystery is great. I walk and yet I am crucified. I am silent yet I shout. I am filled yet hungry, sheltered yet shelterless, warm yet cold, cold yet hot.

What am I? Who am I?

I know — I am everyone, because I love him, my Lord. I am everyone whom he loves, that is my agony. That is my ecstasy. That is who and what I am.

To be everyone for love of him is to participate in the fullness of his passion.   (JI, I)

Christ's desire is to penetrate everyone with his divine life. By becoming Man he has "become everyone" in seed. It is by our identification with the other that his mission is completed. Catherine's hunger is to "be everyone" so that everyone might be filled with Christ.

The following passage is one of Catherine's best descriptions of this mystery of identification. Because of sin, we have separated ourselves from God and from one another. Sin is a refusal of our creaturehood. The journey into poverty is a journey into the reality of our creaturehood, thus making us approachable to one another and able to mediate the love of Christ:

Poverty is not only a virtue. Poverty is a state, a way of life. And this is your first gift to those you come to serve. You can equal their poverty by acknowledging your general poverty as a creature, totally dependent on God. The acceptance of this truth will truly make you free. The more completely you do this — in a mysterious fashion — you will truly identify yourself with those poor. And what is more, by this identification, perhaps unnoticed by everyone, you will heal those very poor you have come to serve.

And so above all he wants you to enter the very heart of poverty because then you will make your poverty a healing, beautiful tool of the apostolate. You will be able to reach beyond the dreams of mankind, and you will enrich Pakistan and the Church's apostolate. You will enrich the Mystical Body in a mysterious and holy fashion. The Crucified, the Naked One, knows his own. He cannot resist the ones who strip themselves naked inwardly for him, who immolate themselves on his own crucifix for love of him and of the souls he died for. Poverty, nakedness, the stripping of self as Jesus did on the Cross. Stripped in this fashion, dying to self, crucified through poverty and obedience, walking in humility, you will be able to feel what the poor feel. You will heal, console, and bring multitudes to God. For you will truly be poor in the full sense of that glorious word, and hence, truly rich.   (SL #148, 1963)

Identification is the key to the opening of our hearts to others:

Our role is identification with everybody because soon everybody will be knocking at the Madonna House door. We will be an oasis for them. If we lose this original spirit of Madonna House we will lose the key to God's heart. God's heart is the only true resting place for all of us, the real oasis to which God calls us. But the key to his heart is identification with himself and with all those he calls his little ones. Don't you see how simple it is!

(Feb., 1977, Unpublished Talk)

It is love, ultimately, which mediates the presence of Christ. Identification, rightly understood, is the essence of love:

Love means an interior and spiritual identification with one's brother, so that he is not regarded as an object to which one does good. Good done to another as an object is of little or no spiritual value. In fact, it is a tragedy which destroys him who does that sort of thing.

Love takes on one's neighbor as one's other self, and loves him with all the immense humility and discretion and reserve and reverence without which no one can presume to enter into the sanctuary of another. From such love, all authoritarianism, brutality, all exploitation, domineering, condescension, must necessarily be absent. The full difficulty and magnitude of the task of loving others should be recognized and never minimized. It is hard to really love others, if love is taken in the full sense of the word.

I have often spoken of identification with the poor. It is an identification that only love can achieve by complete forgetfulness of self and total concern for the other person. It is an identification so deep, so complete, that it becomes part of oneself, like breathing. It is a way of loving.   (FML,159)

Catherine has been given an unusual empathy with the pain of the world:

God of mercy, hear my cry, even though there is no sound. It seems to me the agony of all in agony is mine. It seems to me the pain of all in pain is pounding through my veins. It seems to me I am the lost, the halt, the blind. As if I have left myself behind and become them. God of mercy, hear my cry. Even though it is beyond all human sounds, just as I am beyond all human bounds.

(R, Mar., 1962)

If the whole human race is in pain, how does one alleviate it, how does one help release the love of Christ which alone can heal? The answer is: we do what Christ did. We become the other just as he became Man. In her approach to mission she says exactly that:

> Love identifies itself with those it serves. The whole process is gentle, never violent, never coming from one who thinks himself "better" than the one he teaches or serves. Incarnation is our first step, which is another name for identification, but a more powerful word, one that can shake the foundation of the world, change it, restore it to the Christ whose Incarnation is the motivation of ours.
>
> The process is long, tedious, and painful, but we must change, in a way, into the Hindu we serve, into the African we serve, inasmuch and as far as love will enable us to do so, without any compromise with Christian principles. THIS IS A DEEP INCARNATION AND IT WILL REQUIRE MUCH PRAYER, FASTING, MEDITATION, CONTEMPLATION, AND SILENCE, AS WELL AS WORK AND DYING TO SELF.
>
> But if we succeed in this painful and joyful process . . . the feast of the Transfiguration will enter our life because we have transfigured ourselves as far as it was in our power to do. We have done it out of Love. And because of that love, because of the Incarnation, we have been able, by the grace of God, to truly *preach the Gospel.* I feel sure that he will allow us, then, to be transformed, even as he was transformed. He will allow his light to shine through us as it did through him on Mt. Tabor. (SL #117, 1962)

We arrive here at a turning point in our study. The above quotation expresses the mystical goal of the spiritual life as Catherine understands it. The goal is love, understood as the total emptying of the false self so that one can completely identify with all others. When the emptying is complete, one is then transparent, allowing the transfigured light of Christ to shine through into the lives of others. The whole rest of the Mandate, and all of Catherine's teaching, *is how to do that*. She mentions prayer and fasting and silence, but what she is really saying is that everything else is a *means to this goal*. When you are purified of the false self, you will be able to mediate the presence of the risen, transfigured Christ, who alone can heal the wounds of mankind.

Christ In Pain

And now, we arrive at what I believe is the heart of Catherine's personal spirituality; this book gets its title from this center. For Catherine, the chief means, motivation, reason, passion for the incarnation/identification with others is this: *Christ himself continues to really suffer in his members.* Her passionate love derives not from a "love for mankind" only, or from a desire for "perfection" or "holiness." That too. *But the predominant motivating force in her life is a mystical insight that Christ her Beloved continues to suffer in his members.* First, I will demonstrate this from her writings; secondly, I will give a brief theological basis for this truth:

> You see, for me, night and day, is the face of Christ, the waiting Christ, the lonely Christ, Christ in pain. God knows the world makes him wait. The world leaves him alone in his loneliness. The world forever crucifies him and inflicts on him endless pain. That is killing for me to see.   (SL #105, 1962)

Is this just poetry, the imaginative outpourings of a pious soul? Is it true? Or is it just her "way" which helps her love other people? For Catherine it is literally true, and, if you keep this belief in mind as you read her writings, you will possess the key to them all. Catherine is not simply doing "social work," not simply "helping others along the path of sanctity." She has an acute sense of Christ *now* being in pain, of Christ *now* being lonely and rejected.

Somewhere along her spiritual journey she read Pascal's words which she said were the truest words ever spoken: "Christ is in agony until the end of time." These words illuminated an intuition that God had placed in her heart:

> Christ is in agony until the end of the world. But Christ is in you and me. And what is more important, in the other fellow. What about them being in agony, my brothers and sisters?
>
> That, my friend, is what Madonna House is all about. Open your hearts; you have the key to do it. The Lord has given it to you in baptism. Open your heart and let him in. Stop thinking about yourself and begin — honestly, truthfully, totally — thinking of others.
>
> What does it matter that you and I may become martyrs! That is the crown of faith and Christianity. I doubt if anyone of us, including myself, will have earned it. There is no question of bloody martyrs. There is only the question of slow, white martyrdom. The martyrdom of listening. The martyrdom of consoling. The martyrdom of loving. The martyrdom of hoping, for oneself and for others. The martyrdom of total surrender to God through the other, whoever he or she might be. Prepare yourselves to serve God in totality.
>
> (Family Letter, May, 1980)

All the pain of the world is, in some real sense, also the pain of Christ:

We have to emerge from ourselves. We have to concentrate on the things of the Spirit. We will only be as strong as our life in the Spirit. The time has come for all of us who have been in the apostolate to face the reality of Christ's pain. Behold, that pain is immense. Think of Christ in the world today. Think of him! Meditate on him! Soak yourself in the sight of that pain. Behold, he is the poor, the forgotten, the neglected, the hungry, the cold, the homeless. He is in the thin children with big, old eyes. He is in the restless youth. He is in the alcoholic, the psychopath, the neurotic. You are familiar with this picture of him; you know his pain in these people.

But do you see the pain of Christ in the priests, in the bishops, who spend themselves over and over above all human prudence in trying to assuage that pain of Christ in those who have been crucified? Look with the eyes of your soul. See how he needs you. There is no time to spend on the self that should die so completely so as to make room for him.

Have you seen his pain in the hungry heart of mankind? Have you seen his pain in the rich/poor. Have you seen his pain in the intellectuals of the universities and the schools? Have you seen the pain of Christ in government? Do you feel the horror of the United Nations who are divided because they have not allowed Christ to sit in their councils? Stop, look, behold the pain of Christ! A searing pain that should set your heart on fire, that you might share his pain and become a flame that lights and warms the world. He has allowed you to assuage his pain daily in hundreds of people.   (SL #8, 1956)

I have been thinking about the pain of Christ. Perhaps because Lent is approaching, my mind is turning naturally to the passion of Christ. This same passion continues daily in his Mystical Body. This means in us. Yes, in you and me and in every living human being. And the question rises in my heart: "How do we, children of the Sacred Heart and the Immaculate Heart of his mother, how do we bear — share — his passion in our own minds, bodies, hearts, and souls?" Sharing is the first fruits of his passion; and the second is to assuage, to heal his pain in others.

To share the passion of Christ! To be ready to bear its marks, searing and consuming. Are we ready? Are we ready to die to self so as to forget ourselves? Are we ready to be flagellated, if not with the cat-o-nine-tails, then with whips of evil tongues, uncharitable and thoughtless words! Are we ready to be persecuted by personalities that rub the wounds of our minds and hearts! Are we ready to spend our nights with him in Gethsemane, go with him into the desert, leave father and mother! Are we ready to be stripped naked of self, not caring that we are exposed to the gaze of multitudes who either do not understand us, at best ridicule us, and finally crucify us! Yes, that is what "sharing Christ's passion" means.

Let us answer these questions in the affirmative. Unless we do, unless we really steep ourselves in Christ's passion, identify ourselves with it lovingly, joyously, whole-heartedly, completely, we cannot go forth into the by-ways and alley-ways of the world and seek out the suffering Christ in our brothers. For we will not understand his pain.

Without understanding his pain there is no love, without love there is no healing, no assuaging, no making whole. (SL #10, 1957)

Quotations on this theme could be multiplied hundreds of times. As Catherine says, there are two aspects, or fruits, of this mystery of the ongoing passion of Christ: *sharing* of his pain; then the assuaging (which is also the *healing*) of his pain in others and in oneself. The intuition and living out of this mystery is the foundation of Catherine's life. It is to be presumed in all her writings. It is always present in her heart even though she may not always express it:

> I know that I must pierce my own heart, and die of love. For drop by drop, then, my blood will mingle with his, and this mingling will be the only balm he will take to heal his wounds.   (SL #10, 1957)

It is even more pervasive in her poetic meditations:

> He asked me once, long ago, if I would love him as he loved me. And young and gay and joyous I answered, "Yes indeed!" And then he smiled and instead of a wedding ring he gave me his pain. Since then I have not slept; my soul refused all rest. It was on fire with one desire — to heal his pain. I have become an outcast of love on fire. My desire urges me on. I wonder as I wander: Where shall I find oils and bonds to heal his pain?   (JI, I)

You see the profound faith intuition here? As we enter our own kenosis and suffering, our pain mingles with the pain of Christ. This "mingled suffering" heals both us and the members of the Body; it also comforts Christ in his ongoing agony.

Here are sections of a poem called:

"The Pain Of Christ"

> Have you, beloved friends, felt the pain of Christ which is all around you? It covers me, encompasses me. I cannot rest, cannot be silent before this immense, overwhelming pain of Christ in our brethren.

> I have looked on it for the many years of my lifetime. I have realized too that each year my eyes have seen deeper

into that pain, recognized it faster, wept over it longer, and desired with an ever-growing desire to assuage it sooner.

Yes, I have touched, seen, heard, and slept with the pain of Christ for almost as many years as I have lived. There was a time when I had something to give to assuage this intolerable pain of my God and yours. I had a life to give to it, for it. But now, today, I myself am poor. Behold my poverty. My life I have given, and with it myself, my waking and sleeping hours.

But, Lord of love, it is so little to give, and I stand before you as I am, bereft of any gifts to give while the sea of thy pain rises, rises around me, ever higher. I look to see if there is anything left to give, and I stand before you as I am. Yes, I know I must use it, live it, give it, to bring your pain before the eyes of man.

And so, beloved, friends, here I am, lifting my voice for you to hear — asking, imploring, beseeching for the wherewithal to assuage the pain of Christ in our brethren.   (JI, I)

An Easter Meditation

RABBONI . . . I see You, Gardener of my soul, in splendor clad. . . and yet my heart is heavy . . . for I behold Your beauty unsurpassed in a thousand angry faces . . . and I have EMPTY HANDS!

RABBONI . . . The Alleluias of my joy make jonquil carpets for your pierced feet . . . and yet my heart weeps before the thousand wounds that cover You in the cold and naked who stand so silently before . . . MY EMPTY HANDS!

RABBONI . . . My eyes are dazzled by Your resurrected glory . . . LUMEN CHRISTI . . . and yet my heart beholds the black night of Your loneliness in the forsaken who wait for help from . . . MY EMPTY HANDS!

RABBONI . . . The fragrance of Your unguents brings ecstasy to me . . . yet the bitter-sour smell of Your poverty is wafted to me from the endless line of the pinched, gray faces of the poor. They cry to me from many places, without words. My answer to them is just a display of . . . EMPTY HANDS!

RABBONI . . . Exultant is my soul with songs of gratitude and joy at the conquest of death by You, Lord . . . Yet I see Your blood-stained face so still in Mary's hands . . . in the poor dead! How can I be Your Nicodemus and bury them with EMPTY HANDS!

RABBONI . . . WILL YOU ONCE MORE ENTER THROUGH THE CLOSED DOOR OF HUMAN HEARTS . . . AND SHOW THEM YOUR WOUNDS? YOUR PIERCED AND LOVING HEART? AND MAKE THEM SEE THEY STILL MUST BELIEVE YOUR WORDS . . . AND YOU? FOR YOU HAVE SAID . . . THAT ALL THAT IS DONE TO THE LEAST OF YOUR BRETHREN IS DONE TO YOU! THEN . . . PERHAPS . . . THEY WILL OPEN THEIR HEARTS AND PURSES . . . AND FILL MY EMPTY HANDS . . . WITH SILVER AND GOLD THAT WILL ALLOW US TO — FEED THE HUNGRY . . . CLOTHE THE NAKED . . . HOUSE THE FORSAKEN . . . BURY THE DEAD.

RABBONI . . . PLEASE?   (JI, I)

Oh, Christ

Oh Christ of the forgotten, the sick, the halt, the blind.

Oh Christ of the lonely missions and the jungle of city street.

Behold me weeping before your need — in them!

Oh Jesus, Son of Mary, give me your grace abundantly.

Make my small voice heard, proclaiming to all who love you, your urgent need of them.

Oh divine Beggar, give me the strength to beg for you until the very end.

For Christ of the forgotten, I need silver and gold to purchase the wine and oil of charity supreme.

The charity that alone will fill your needs in all the poor, sick, lame, halt, blind, and forgotten, and still *your pain in them.* (JI, I)

This desire to share and assuage the pain of Christ in his members is, without a doubt, the central inspiration behind Catherine's passionate love for Christ.

CHAPTER SIX

Assuaging
The Loneliness Of Christ

* * *

Of all the various kinds of sufferings undergone by
Christ in his members — physical pain, rejection, in-
gratitude — there is one kind of pain more central for
Catherine than all the others: *loneliness.* I will demonstrate
this from her writings, and then try to answer the question
why this should be so.

On the first page of "Our Way of Life" Catherine
quotes the following poem (not her own) which spoke
deeply to her heart from the first time she read it. The fact
that she included it in our Constitution, and put it on the
very first page, signifies its importance for her and her
spirituality:

> I said, 'Let me work in the fields.' Christ said, 'No, work
> in the town.'
>
> I said, 'There are no flowers there.' He said, 'No flowers,
> but a crown.'
>
> I said, 'But the sky is dark, and there is nothing but noise
> and din.'

Christ wept as he answered back, 'There is more, there
is sin.'

I said, 'I shall miss the lights, and friends will miss me,
they say.'

Christ answered, 'Choose tonight, if I shall miss you, or
they.' (WL)

Often during spiritual readings after lunch, Catherine
would ask for her book of poems. I think the poem she read
to us most frequently is the following.

It really expresses the very heart of the Little Mandate:

O lonely Christ of Charing Cross, Rue de la Paix,
Boulevard Anspach,
O lonely Christ of a thousand celebrated thoroughfares
and foreign-sounding streets.
Why is it that I have to meet you here, so far from home,
Where I have seen you lonely, too, in Harlem and Fifth
Avenue?
In Edmonton, Yukon, Portland Oregon, Chicago,
San Francisco, Kalamazoo
You were lonely too.

O lonely Christ of everywhere,
Why stand there . . . and here . . .
So still, so sad, looking at the hurrying crowds pass you by?
Why? Why are your eyes so full of hunger, longing, pity
and compassion?
Why do you lift your nail-torn hand, and then let it fall
again,
With so much sadness . . . as if you were a beggar about to
beg, alas!

Why is it that I have to meet you across all continents,
All celebrated thoroughfares, strange, dingy streets and
palatial avenues,

As well as wild and distant places?
You answer nothing: you just look.

O Christ of Charing Cross, so lonely.
You weep because the multitudes are hungry
for your love and know it not.
And because you hunger to be loved by those who know
you not.

Give me the key, Beloved, so that I may open your
loneliness
And . . . entering . . . share its weight.
Behold my heart that you have wounded with your love.
Make it a door for all to come to you.
Give me your voice and words of fire
That I may show them *you!*   (JI, I)

If I were asked to choose a few brief lines from
Catherine's writings which express the heart of her personal
spiritual life, I would pick the last few lines of this poem.
First, she asks for the grace to enter Christ's own heart to
share his loneliness. Then, wounded by that immense love
for her, she asks that she might in turn become an open door
through which people pass to discover that same love. She
asks Christ for words of fire to invite them to his banquet of
love. The rest of the Mandate concerns *how to accomplish this
openness of heart so others may be comforted; as they are comforted,
Christ in his loneliness is comforted also.*

In December, 1957, Catherine wrote a Christmas letter
to her spiritual family. She said: "You remember my little
letter poem, 'The Lonely Christ of Charing Cross'? Well,
this is Chapter Two of that poem." The letter is not too long.
I'm going to quote it in its entirety, because this theme really
is for Catherine the heart of her heart, the soul of her soul:

Before my eyes — all through this Advent and poignantly now, as his birthday approaches — is a strange picture of Christ's loneliness. In a few days we can well imagine that he will be born again in Bethlehem, in all the endless Bethlehems in all our towns, villages, and hamlets. The angels will be singing there, but somehow I do not see the shepherds!

Millions and millions of people will not raise their voices to God for him to hear, nor make the cold of the season warm, nor decorate a "stable" with their love. Millions and millions either do not know he is being born, or knowing, do not care; and lastly, the tragic thought: knowing-*hate*. How intense must be the loneliness of Christ in Bethlehem in the year 1957!

And it goes on. The flight into Egypt. The members of the Holy Family were the first refugees of the Christian era. Was there anyone to care, to help, to console? Probably at the time there was, but what about today? How many thousands of Christs are forgotten in the refugee camps? How many more thousands have been exiled, have taken the same flight into Egypt — and have found it desert because we do not love them enough! How lonely is the exiled Christ, Christ the Refugee, in our day!

And then, my spirit falters before the loneliness of Nazareth. The Creator subject to his creature. God the Ineffable, the Incomprehensible, out of love imprisoning himself in our human flesh, working with his hands. He whose word could build a universe, whose thought could produce a tree or a forest, painstakingly shaves a board with a plane.

The fluttering of the woodshavings on the floor must have been a lonely sound to him even then. And how about now? I feel the loneliness of all the lonely ones in the world. It might not be the fluttering sound of wood shavings on the floor. It might be the sound of laughter on the street, overheard in some room in a boarding house. It might be the sound of a kiss outside the window, the kiss of a woman wondering about the love of her husband.

There are so many sounds heard everywhere by the lonely Christ in so many lonely hearts, souls, minds, the world over. I shiver a little as I think of it. Don't you?

And the loneliness of his public life, when perhaps only the spring and summer breeze caught his holy words. These winds carried his words across the face of the earth.

How many millions hear his words today and do nothing about them, letting them fall flat, fallow, dead, before they do anything about them! How many have ears and hear not? How lonely must be the Christ of our day as he continues his public ministry and sees the shrinking crowds and the shrinking priestly vocations.

The loneliness of Gethsemane, with its terrific mental suffering, its agony of mind and heart and soul. It affected him so much that sweaty drops of blood came forth. How many thousands are in Gethsemane now. The alcoholics, the psychotics, the neurotics, each spelling in their lonely lives — laboriously, agonizingly, painfully — each letter of the word "GETHSEMANE"!

And finally, the loneliness of the Crucified upon the Cross. The loneliness of Golgotha. From how many Golgothas does Christ look down upon the world today? The crucified ones behind the Iron and Bamboo curtains. Those crucified in our very midst among the hustle and bustle of Christmas shopping and preparations. The poor, the sick, the suffering!

And then the crowning of loneliness — the tomb! Alone, cold, with a heavy stone rolled in front of its emptiness. The lonely ones in prison. Perhaps they have suffered all the loneliness that I have tried so poorly to describe.

One could go on and on, entering the infinite depths of Christ's loneliness in his Mystical Body in our day. But what would be the reason for entering those depths, unless they brought us to the heights of Christmas, its joy and love?

We must remember, in our apostolate, that its essence IS TO SMASH THE LONELINESS OF CHRIST, TO ASSUAGE IT, TO SHARE IT.

In a few days we shall kneel at the Crib. Let our hands be filled with the desire to do so, that is, assuage the loneliness of Christ. And let us pray to this Little Christmas Infant before whom we kneel to give us the grace to implement this desire into the reality of our daily life.

Lovingly yours in the Lonely Christ,

CATHERINE
(SL #15, 1957)

Christ continues to suffer his passion of loneliness in all the suffering people of our day. When Catherine says it's the essence of our apostolate to smash, assuage, and share the loneliness of Christ, she is saying that it is also the heart of her own life. Her poem, "I Bleed For Love":

I love the souls of men so much that if it were needed I
would go back again and die.
But I am condemned, it seems, by the free will of men.
Me, condemned to loneliness.
I am a Beggar — not for any of the goods of this world —
but a Beggar for your love.   (JI, I)

Nor is this theme confined to "an early stage" of Catherine's life. In 1979, she wrote:

I want this year of 1979 to be a year of consolation of our Lord by Madonna House staff. Let us forget the word "I." Let us forget our difficulties. Let us remember . . . that we are third. God is first, our neighbor is second. I want this year to be the year of the Lord. Let us remember him. Let us think of him. He will need consolation in us, dearly beloved, he will need consolation in us. Always pray! Serve by listening. Serve by consoling. Serve by wiping the tears of children, men and women. This is really to console Christ in Gethsemane. When you serve each other — the poor in any way, shape or form — you are wiping his face, you are carrying his cross, you are in Gethsemane, consoling him! (SL #109, 1962)

In a series of articles written in 1980 entitled, "Madonna House, What Is It?" she wrote, in the prophetic voice:

It was not easy for me to be rejected by men whom I
   had come to serve.
I was lonely.
Even my apostles did not understand very well.
It is because I want Madonna House to follow in my
   footsteps that I allow them to share in my loneliness.
Direct them to my loneliness. (MHWII)

Many more examples could be cited. As I go through her writings on the Mandate, notice how often the ultimate goal of her heart's intention is to comfort Christ, to become a crib wherein he may rest, to assuage his pain by her pain, experienced in the multiple forms of human existence. Catherine is always relating directly to Christ in every one of her actions. This is the great key to her passionate life of love.

Why Loneliness?

Why the loneliness of Christ? Why not his rejection, his physical pain, his frustration? Besides the ever-mysterious grace of the Holy Spirit (which is the final explanation), I offer several brief reasons which have certainly contributed to Catherine's seeing Christ par excellence as the Lonely One.

Arseniev begins the summary of his book, *Russian Piety*, with the words: "The Russians are a very lonely people." He goes on to describe how isolated Russians have been from the rest of the world. Is there a deep sense of loneliness in their national religious psyche?

Secondly, Catherine's own life experiences would be more than enough to explain this emphasis. Practically overnight she lost her country forever; she never returned to Russia. Exiled from her homeland (and remember how sacred and dear the Land, Mother Russia, is to a true Russian), a refugee and "foreigner" in the new world, it is no wonder she often described herself as a "stranger in a strange land."

Thirdly, I believe the depth of a person's life with God increases the sense of aloneness. Compounded with that is Catherine's clearly prophetic vocation. Prophets often must stand alone, as she often did on the major issues of the day.

Finally, I think it is a valid theological thesis that loneliness just may be the deepest wound of our disorientation from God. If we were made for union, then non-union, isolation, separation, would be the deepest pain. Isn't it true that suffering in communion with others is more bearable than suffering alone? But when aloneness is *the suffering*, the darkness can be unfathomable. Jesus' cry on the Cross was a cry of abandonment and loneliness: "Father, where are you?" It is the ongoing depths of this loneliness of Christ on the Cross that Catherine seeks to assuage by her love.

Loneliness

Loneliness like a beast is tearing at my heart and succeeding in tearing it apart. How can I live, O Lord of the pierced Heart, when all I have is bleeding morsels for a heart?

Loneliness, like some obscene old woman who prostituted her youth for shillings, pence, rupees, cents, cackles night and day into my ears until my mind weeps silently and hopelessly its bloody tears.

Loneliness comes to me like a ghostly thing, like a skeleton from a thousand graves, embracing me like lovers do in the dark night.

Loneliness sings to me its ghastly lullabies that keep all sleep from me night after night until the sound of it, the sight of it, drives me into surrealistic, frightening dreams without sleep!   (JI, I)

The Theology Of Christ's Ongoing Pain

Because of the importance of this theme of Catherine's spirituality, I want to pause here and give a brief theological explanation of Christ's ongoing suffering in his members. This is not Catherine's explanation, but my own. She does not, herself, go into the theological foundations of her thought. She reads theology, and is a very sound theologian, I believe. But she would leave to others the elaboration of the deeper theological foundations of her thought.

"Christ is in pain until the end of time." Is this good theology, or mere pious thoughts to motivate our love for

Christ? Christ is in heaven, isn't he? How can he be in any real pain? Pius XII, in his great encyclical, *On the Mystical Body*, wrote:

> He (Christ) is the Head of the Body of the Church (Col 1:18). And the unbroken tradition of the Fathers from the earliest times teaches that the Divine Redeemer and the Society which is his Body form but one mystical Body, that is to say, to quote St. Augustine, the whole Christ. Our Savior Himself in his sacerdotal prayer did not hesitate to liken this union to that wonderful unity by which the Son is in the Father, and the Father in the Son. (#67)

> In the crib, on the Cross, in the unending glory of the Father, Christ has all the members of the Church present before Him, and united to Him in a much clearer and more loving manner than that of a mother who clasps her child to her breast, or than that with which a man knows and loves himself. (#75)

> Let those weighty words of Our immortal predecessor Leo the Great be deeply engraven upon our minds, that by "Baptism we are made the flesh of the Crucified." (#108)

I don't think anyone has any difficulty with an interpretation of this mystery of the suffering of Christ in his members which has been made in hundreds of spiritual books throughout the ages, namely, that when Jesus was suffering in the Garden and on Calvary, he *foresaw* both the sins of the whole world and the love of people for him. Our sins added to his sufferings, and our love consoled and comforted him. I think this is one approach to the question.

But I think the theological truth is even deeper than this. Pius XII speaks of our union with Christ *now* in his unending glory with the Father. Emile Mersch, in his great classic study, *The Theology of the Mystical Body*, writes:

Jesus often speaks of His 'body' as though it were a suffering and dying organism (Mt 25:31), and the only words He uttered on the subject after His ascension . . . disclose that the body will always suffer the same persecutions as He himself: "Saul, Saul, why persecutest thou Me?" (p. 395)

In *The Ascension in the Works of St. Augustine*, Father Marrevee writes:

Even if the Head is in heaven, his unity with the members means that He is still persecuted Himself. Augustine finds this unity in tribulations most clearly expressed in the words to Saul on his way to Damascus: "Saul, Saul, why do you persecute me?" and in Christ's words, "I tell you, in so far as you did it to one of the humblest of these brothers of mine, you did it to me."

"And when he said, 'Saul, Saul . . .' the head is crying out for the members. He does not say, 'Why are you persecuting my members,' but 'Why are you persecuting me.'" (In Ps 39)

"Christ indeed ascended on high, and is sitting at the right of the Father, but unless he were also not right here on earth he could not have cried, 'Saul, Saul, Saul . . .' When, therefore, he says the same thing, 'What you do to one of my little ones you do to me,' can we doubt he accepts into his members the gift his members accept?" (In Ps 67)

When, therefore, he insists, on the one hand, that there is a clear distinction between the present situation of Christ as Head and the Church as His Body, he finds on the other hand in the intimate union between them grounds for ascribing exaltation and suffering to both the Head and the Body. The fact that Christ is exalted does not mean that He remains unmoved as Head by the troubles which His Body in exile must endure.

"The Head about to ascend into heaven commended to us His members on earth and departed. Thenceforth you do not find Christ speaking on earth; you find him speaking from Heaven. Why? Because his members on earth were trodden upon. For to the persecutor Saul he said, 'Saul, Saul, why do you persecute me? I am ascended into heaven, but still lie on earth; here I sit at the right hand of the Father, but there I yet hunger, thirst, and am a stranger!' "   (In Ep. John)

And this from the Roman Breviary from a sermon of St. Augustine on the Ascension:

For just as he remained with us after his Ascension, so we too are already in heaven with him, even though what is promised us has not yet been fulfilled in our bodies.

Christ is now exalted above the heavens, but he still suffers on earth all the pain that we, the members of his body, have to bear. He showed this when he cried out from above: "Saul, Saul, why do you persecute me?" And when he said, "I was hungry and you gave me food."

While in heaven he is also with us, and we, while on earth, are with him. These words are explained by our oneness with Christ, for he is our head and we are his body. Out of compassion for us he ascended to heaven, and although he ascended alone, we also ascend, because we are in him by grace. The body as a unity cannot be separated from the head.

These statements by one of the greatest doctors of the Church seem to me to be very clear and unambiguous. What we probably need to revise is our concept of heaven and the state of the blessed.

Allow me to quote one brief passage from the Eastern tradition on this aspect of the mystery of the Incarnation. It is from Maximus the Confessor. It is a perfect statement of the heart of Catherine's spirituality. Note the reference both to the ongoing passion of Christ and to our own "becoming God" by curing the sufferings of others through Christ's power:

> If, as He has said (referring to 2 Cor 8:9), God is the poor one in making Himself poor in condescension for us, in accepting for Himself in compassion the sufferings of the others, *and in suffering mystically out of goodness until the end of time according to the measure of suffering of everyone,* even more obviously will he become God who, imitating the divine philanthropy, cures through Himself in a divine manner the sufferings of the suffering, and who manifests in his attitude the same power as God, in the analogy of the providence of salvation.   (Italics mine)
> Thunberg, *Man and the Cosmos*, p. 66

Finally, apropos of the loneliness theme in Catherine's spirituality, Mersch says this:

> Christ alone has suffered in solitude, without other support than God, who sustained Him at that hour so that He might suffer more intensely. He alone was engaged in the task at the moment when sinners were as yet no more than sinners, at the moment of unmitigated pain and pure redemption.   (p. 315)

I think that Christ's cry on the cross is the expression of the profoundest limit of his kenosis: as much as it was possible for him to experience the absence of his Father, he did. Absolutely no one was with him in that abandonment.

And even though his Mother was there, not even she could enter these depths with him.

Catherine's whole spirituality is a passion to assuage this abandonment, this loneliness, of Christ. This pain continues in us, his members. It is assuaged through our own painful kenosis as we open our hearts to others. To refuse this cross is to leave Christ alone in his abandonment. In the second line of the Mandate we begin our journey on *how to assuage the ongoing loneliness of Christ.*

CHAPTER SEVEN

Childlikeness

* * *

Little — Be Always Little — Childlike

So, we're on an immense journey into the fire of the Holy Three, into the mystery of the hidden life of Nazareth, into the holiness of Mother Church. We pilgrimage, holding onto Mary's hand as she teaches us how to walk by faith and the spirit of the beatitudes. The call to "Arise!" sounds in our ears at every moment as we seek the face of the courageous Pilgrim, Christ.

Like all real adventures it is fearsome, intriguing, full of both pitfalls and wonderful surprises. We walk with great reverence into the poor heart of every person, guided by this baffling Lady Poverty who was born from the depths of Christ's own kenosis on the Cross. If you are a true adventurer and not a comfortable modern traveler, the journey will have its pain and anguish. To be in our broken world, seeking the Father's face, is necessarily to be on a path of suffering.

But there will be no place of terror Jesus has not penetrated before us. If we join our heart to his Heart, we conquer our fears, keep him company in his ongoing passion, and co-operate with him in banishing darkness from the world. If we keep walking with Christ and Our Lady, we will discover our own loneliness being transformed into communion; also, we will assuage the loneliness of the Lonely Christ in others.

I've already quoted a part of what Catherine says about this second line. She was seeking a "deeper meaning of the first paragraph of the Little Mandate. Two ideas of poverty were working themselves out in my soul: one physical and geographical; the other transcendent and difficult to get a hold of . . . an inner sort of poverty, a detachment . . . a giving of one's inner self with childlike trust." She says that this line is "the most difficult part of the Mandate"   (HMCB).

This second line is the most difficult because it concerns *states of being*, or rather, various aspects of our fundamental state of being before God. Catherine constantly calls us to "being before doing": "What you do matters — but not much! What you *are* matters tremendously."

Look at the other lines of the Mandate for a moment. Except for "be hidden . . . be a light" they are all calls to *do* something. But it is not possible to *do* any of these things unless our activity flows from a new depth of *being*. The activities can and do increase and deepen our state of being, but only insofar as we keep our hearts childlike, simple, little, and spiritually poor.

I'm going to begin with the theme of childlikeness because I believe it is biblically the richest description of the "being-goal" to which we are tending.

What is our deepest reality? It is to be like Jesus who was the perfect Child of the Father. Childlikeness for the Christian is not optional; it is not one type of spirituality among others. Jesus says, "*Unless* you become like children." A very sound and accurate biblical way of understanding the *personal goal* of our pilgrimage is this: We are seeking to return to, have restored to us, our true heritage as *children of the Father.*

Bethlehem

As soon as we "touch down" upon the earth we begin to be conditioned by the "sin of the world" and "original sin." As we "grow up" we also "grow away" from our Father, more or less, depending upon many circumstances. When we begin in earnest our free and conscious return to the Father, it acquires, biblically, the characteristics of a journey towards spiritual childhood. Mary is the perfect one to accompany us, because, as she "grew up," she never "grew away" from the Father. Her sinlessness means that she always was becoming more and more the daughter of the Father. *Bethlehem* is Catherine's symbol for this goal of perfect childlikeness:

Christmas 1969

In the dark night I heard a voice:

"Where are you going restless one,
who stands so still, yet pilgrims unceasingly?"

I answered: "I journey always to Bethlehem,
to ask The Child for the gift of childlikeness."

"But do you know that you must go through burning
jungles beset by traps and napalm?"

I answered: "Yes, I know, that is why I go . . .
For only he who seeks The Child can go through
fire, beasts, traps, and napalm, to find The Child." (JI, I)

This immense pilgrimage is fraught with dangers. Only one really seeking the Child will have the necessary courage.

Christ, the Beloved, is called "The Child" here because this is the depth of identification we are seeking with him: to become the perfect child of the Father, as he is.

In the following poem we have the theme of the consolation of Christ joined with that of becoming a child: if we become childlike, we become a manger for him, making up for the neglect of so many:

Advent 1961

I sought a woman's womb to become Man. Now I seek a soul to bring my love to them!

A soul to become my stable, my manger, my Bethlehem!

So I take thy poverty into my descending and *fill it to the brim.* Have faith! Have love!

Let my winds and waters fill you up!

You will return and find me within your soul and heart — simple and humble — a child.   (JI, I)

In her earlier writings Catherine often joined Bethlehem and Nazareth together, because they were both powerful symbols of the heart of her spirituality:

Let us enter the school of Bethlehem and Nazareth, to grow in the one thing that matters — love. And since we are so little, let us learn in that school of charity, which is Bethlehem and Nazareth, the little things that make his charity great. Let us be small, humble, poor . . . ready to go where we are sent . . . making our home in Bethlehem and Nazareth, now and forever.   (SL #34, 1958)

Bethlehem and Nazareth are together because both deeply concern childlikeness, hiddenness and simplicity.

Along the way, Catherine herself grew into a deeper clarification of the respective places of these mysteries. Since Catherine sees the life of Christ as a pattern for her own, Bethlehem is where the journey inward *begins.* Secondly, life can be conceived as a journey *from Bethlehem* to Calvary. Thirdly, because we are seeking the restoration of our image as perfect children of the Father, Bethlehem is also the *final goal* towards which we journey. A brief presentation of each of these aspects.

The journey *begins* in Bethlehem:

> It is a very simple journey, this Journey Inward that each lay apostle takes in order to make the Lay Apostolate the true success it must be. It is like God's journey Outward from heaven to Bethlehem; from Bethlehem to Nazareth; from Nazareth to Calvary. The Lay Apostolate starts at Bethlehem. Small, humble, unknown — like the hamlet — the lay apostle gives birth to God.
>
> From now on he will begin to die to self, so as to be filled with Christ and be able to say with St. Paul — "I live now, not I, but Christ liveth in me." (R, Dec., 1947)

This is a very early part of Catherine's thinking, and goes back farther than 1947; it was written originally for *Friendship House News.*

Since we are to model our life on that of Christ, we can also conceive of our earthly journey as a pilgrimage *from* Bethlehem to Calvary:

> He came because he loved us. His Father sent him because he loved us. Eventually he would tell us about the Holy Spirit who also loves us and will guide us.
>
> But now, on the horizon, stands a cross, and we should realize that through our whole life we are pilgrimaging from the creche to the cross.

What does this mean, this life-long pilgrimage of ours? It means, or should mean, that year after year, we enter deeper and deeper into his lifestyle. That we take for our own the poverty of the cross.   (R, Feb., 1976)

In a very early articulation of the Mandate Catherine wrote:

The Spirit of the Madonna House Institute is one of childlike simplicity. To be childlike and simple means not to evade Calvary. Childlike simplicity faces the very simple fact that there is no evading the cross, and being crucified on it and dying to self. For only thus can we love Him back.

So away with all the tortuous arguments! We are walking from where we are now to that cross, without deviating from that direct path. That is what is meant by childlike simplicity in its most fundamental and simple form.
(SL #38, 1959)

And in a Christmas Letter for 1976:

When we reach Bethlehem our heart will fall and adore him quite naturally. We will understand, while we stand there, how the creche, made of wood, blends with the cross which has also been made of wood. And in standing before the Child in that creche (that will change its shape in time to come) we will understand that this is our life too. We too are in a creche; we too are really journeying to a cross; we too follow in his footsteps.

And so, my dearly beloved, it might not be a long Christmas letter, but it comes to you from my heart. I shall journey with you to Bethlehem. Together we shall walk on the journey from Bethlehem to Golgotha. Together we shall know once again (although we already know) that we live in the resurrected Christ.

And as you see, there is an essence that I want to give you. I want to give you the desire of the Desired One. But I also want to give you childlikeness. It's impossible not to be childlike with the Child Jesus. (SLFF #75, 1976)

So it's true to say that Bethlehem is both the place where we begin, because that's where Christ began, and also the place to which we are journeying, because it symbolizes our return to childlikeness.

Catherine has a great devotion to the Infant Jesus. His Incarnation as a Baby was the first great manifestation of his kenosis for love of us. One of her favorite prayers (which is on the wall of the Madonna House chapel) is: "Give me the heart of a child and the awesome courage to live it out." The "Arise-Go!" is a pilgrimage to our becoming a child of the Father as Christ told us to do. Catherine equates this with sanctity: "I equate maturity with sanctity . . . and maturity and sanctity mean childlikeness." (LDM, 1978)

The Passion Of The Infant Christ

Christ began his journey as a Child in the creche, but he was neglected and unknown by the world. Thus the ongoing passion of Christ continues in the Child of Bethlehem who suffers this neglect and unwantedness in the world today. This theme appears mostly in Catherine's meditations for Christmas:

If we open the ears of our souls we can hear the Child cry again, even in the noise of our machines . . . for this is God crying, God who made himself Man for love of us. (R, Dec., 1962)

So often a new-born Child cries alone, with only a few hearts ready to become a crib for him . . . with only a few souls ready to pick him up and sing him a lullaby of their love. Only a few ears hear his pleading cry.

(R, Dec., 1959)

Yes, let us arise and go on a pilgrimage to the million Bethlehems across the endless expanse of our earth . . . It won't be necessary to leave our homes to go on such a pilgrimage of prayer and atonement. One thing will be necessary this Christmas — that we strip ourselves of all we don't need and bring it to the feet of the poor.

(R, Dec., 1971)

It is time . . . for us rich nations and well-to-do individuals to make a collective and individual examination of conscience. Unless we do we shall not find our way to the cave of Bethlehem. Our hands will be empty of all gifts that we could have given to the Child who is in our brothers everywhere.   (R, Dec., 1969)

The pain and suffering, the passion of Christ, is alive and exists across the world today. Men are . . . still being hunted and tortured. These men are our brothers . . . because a Child was born in Bethlehem . . . and that Child was God.   (R, Dec., 1968)

Child In Pain Christmas — 1972

Suddenly, Bethlehem was in our midst — in the alley with the garbage, in the hospital of abortion, in the foundling wrapped in red tape.

Yes, suddenly Bethlehem — Manger and cave — were here and You came with them.   (JI, II)

Lonely Christ Of Bethlehem

Oh Lonely Christ of Bethlehem,
Of Egypt's flight to Nazareth,
Where are the shepherds, where is their song?

You go and go, my lonely Christ,
From DP camp to DP camp,
Until you die without dying,
In the red tape of our denying.   (JI, II)

The Christ Child

At night I come to you!
Beseeching of your Majesty
Just one gift for me.

The gift of making men see your poverty,
Eternally renewed in endless stables, cold and dark,
Across our fair and immense land.   (JI, II)

And finally, the moving and poignant outpourings of a
mother's heart to comfort the Child:

Christmas Lullaby

The night was clear, the winds were cold, the Baby
cried.
Hush, Baby, Hush.
Here is a quilt made just for you, out of the thousand
little things we do.
Hush, Baby, Hush.

The night was clear, the frost was bitter,
The frost was fierce, the Baby cried.
Hush, Baby, Hush.
We'll make you a fire of all our desires.
Hush, Baby, Hush.

The night was dark, the snow fell in large,
White flakes.
It covered forests, covered lakes, the Baby cried.
Hush, Baby, Hush.

We'll melt the snow, we'll make it glow,
With our hearts so filled with love for you.
Hush, Baby, Hush. (JI, II)

God as a Baby is Catherine's starting point for her passionate love, for her understanding of kenosis. She is rapt in
awe at the helplessness and littleness of the Infinite:

A Child

Splendor, fire, all desire, absorbed, reflected, in a
Child.
Wood, straw, a Child, Lone within reach.
Little, small, like a doll.

Immense, infinite, Bridegroom — God!
Wood, nails, Man, Love fulfilled.

My soul is mute; I don't exist!
For I am lost, absorbed, dissolved,
In the glory of a Child's eyes.

Behold, One I can hold in my arms! (JI, II)

The Lord said, "I am . . . the truth." In the following
excerpt we have a good example of how Catherine weaves
her many themes in ever more intricate and beautiful patterns: Truth is a Child; the Child is in Bethlehem; and only
Mary can lead us to him because he came through her; and
to go to Bethlehem you must be humble and little and
simple.

Truth Is A Child

Truth is a child, born in Bethlehem,
Mary is the lock, the latch, the key.
You will not see the child,
Unless you pass thru Her.

Perhaps you think it dwells on mountains high,
And you a mountaineer of great prowess.
Do not ascend; descend in humility.
Then, when you have walked its narrow road —
a lane, you will find a crossroad. Turn right.
The trail is faint, but oh! how bright.
For you are walking the road of simplicity.

Come, I will show you where truth dwells.
It is a Child. Fear not, if you have sinned.
If you walk in humility, simplicity, and with
the staff of poverty of spirit.
All you have to bring is tears.

But if you go with me, let us start in search
of Truth in Palestine.
There in a cave, behind an inn, with door quite low.
(But poor folks are used to bowing quite low.)
And there we will meet Her, not very tall but stately.
She will ask us what we seek, and we will say,
Quite simply, "God, Your Son, to know, to adore,
to love, to serve, to live, to die, for Him."

Childlike Virtues

All the virtues, remember, are aspects of the poverty/
love movement towards God, the emptying so as to be filled
with Christ. Some virtues more than others are closely allied
with childlikeness, with the attitude of a child before the
Father.

Running To Abba

Modern man has "come of age." We have ceased being
dependent on the great father-image in the sky. Certainly
there is a wrong way of depending on God, or expecting

God to do things he has given us the grace and even command to do. In the following passage, Catherine is not speaking of false dependence. She of all people used all her talents in the service of God. But what she reveals here is that her real strength and confidence and surety come from God. She does not trust in her own strength and wisdom to meet life's demands.

> I get irritated, miserable, when I don't run to my father, when I don't remember that I am little, when I don't say, "ABBA," but say: "Now, Katie, you are a pretty brilliant dame. You've known this apostolate for 39 years. Okay, I'll solve this problem."

> But if I run to my Father, and take his hand, and cry "ABBA," and become very small, realizing I can solve nothing . . . then the big, bad dog, which seemed the size of a mountain in Switzerland, suddenly becomes the size of a pekinese. My Father solves the problem, because I was childlike, and I approached the problem in a childlike fashion, instead of in the pride of my intellect.

> Being little, always little, being small, being poor, being childlike, will solve every problem. So you have a terrible problem in your house. Remember, you're poor. Do not be ashamed to be a failure. What do you expect! If the Son of God saved us through a failure, then why can't you save the world by failure too? At least your little world. I thank God for showing me that I am poor. Which is what our Little Mandate tells us.   (TOLM)

Trust

Materially, a child is totally dependent upon its parents for everything. Our material dependencies — food, air, the beating of our hearts — are symbols of our absolute dependency on God for our very existence.

For beggars cannot be choosers. They cut their lives to fit the cloth according to the gifts of charity that others give them. They have nothing of their own, and so are dependent totally on the providence of God. This brings about an increase of faith and love for the Almighty. The Fatherhood of God, up until now a tenet of a somewhat academic faith, becomes a reality of everyday living. Now the Gospel of the lilies of the field and the birds of the air makes sense! Now one truly is a brother or sister of Christ, and a child of our Father who is in heaven.

(SL #94, 1962)

Openness And Defenselessness

Closely allied to this absolute trust is the openness and spontaneity of a child. Also, a child has not yet built up the defenses of adulthood. In a small child, of course, these are not really virtues. Our growth into spiritual childhood is to acquire the openness and spontaneity and defenselessness as mature virtues of the conscious Christian:

Trust belongs to those who have the heart of a child. That's why I have such a great devotion to the Infant. The Infant represents to me childlikeness which is what Christ said is the key to the kingdom of heaven. So, trust among us must be complete, otherwise we cannot move, we cannot grow.

With trust goes a deep understanding of what . . . openness is. A child is open. He talks to his father and mother about everything and anything. Yes, openness, defenselessness, these all belong to Madonna House and are part and parcel of its very life. (MHWII, #26)

Sense Of Wonder And Celebration

For a small child everything is new and filled with wonder and amazement. "Adults" become accustomed to wonders. Chesterton says that if a door opens and someone comes in, the adult pays attention to the person, whereas the child is amazed with the door opening!

> Celebration is a return to childhood. It is simply the ability to begin to wonder again. It takes the eyes of a child to see that, and it takes the eyes of a child to wonder and to feel within his soul the music of celebration.
>
> (SL #52, 1975)

In the 19th century much of religion was defined in terms of immature dependence. To "grow up," the human person had to "outgrow" these dependencies. Karl Stern, in *Flight From Woman*, says that because of this false attitude the Holy Spirit has raised up people like the Little Flower, with her wonderful doctrine of true spiritual childhood, to again teach the world how to be "maturely dependent before the Father" (p. 296).

Catherine also seeks to foster true dependency in contrast to childishness in religion. St. Paul reminds us that it *is* possible to remain *childish* in our life with God:

> When I was a child, I used to talk like a child, think like a child, reason like a child; when I became a man, I put childish ways aside.   (1 Cor 13:11)

Sin can also distort our concept of childlikeness. Nevertheless, there is a trust, an openness, a dependency, a defenselessness which, if guided by the Spirit, are absolutely essential to the restoration of the divine image of the Child within us.

Little — Be Always Little

The first paragraph of the Mandate, remember, is the heart, the "central word," you might say. This is the word that knocked her off her horse! This is the word which opened the heavens for her (Ezk 1:1). This is the word the Lord spoke to her when, like Samuel, she finally realized it *was* the Lord, and she said with all her heart:

"Speak, Lord, your servant is listening" (1 S 3:9).

After every real, authentic encounter with the Lord the creature's first reaction is one of unworthiness, insignificance: "Depart from me, O Lord, for I am a sinful man"; "I am too young, I cannot speak"; "Who am I that the mother of my Lord should come to me?" Catherine believes that she is really being called by God to meet Christ in the heart of the poor, and that this call has immense significance not only for herself but for others as well. Realizing the awesomeness of this call, her first response is: "I must become very little, very simple, very poor — like a child." It is the response of humility, the only attitude which can allow God to accomplish all he wishes through those he elects: "Behold the handmaid of the Lord."

Frequently in the Scriptures — not to say almost invariably — God chooses the smallest and weakest to accomplish his designs. Israel, Joseph, Bethlehem, David — they are all the smallest, the youngest, the weakest. It is crucial to the fruitfulness of their mission that they never forget this: "If Yahweh set his heart on you and chose you, it was not because you were the greatest of all the people — you were the smallest of all the people — but because Yahweh loved you . . ." (Dt 7:7). St. Paul spoke of himself as "the least of the apostles" (1 Cor 15:9) and "the least of all God's people"

(Ep 3:7). I believe, then, that the words in this line flow from her awarenesss of having been chosen by God for a great work. For this work to be accomplished one must remain/become little, simple, poor, childlike, so that the grace of God may not encounter any obstacle. What follows are some of the important meanings of "littleness" for Catherine.

Chosen

Catherine had an early and ever-deepening awareness of having been *chosen* by God for a special work. In the light of such an election, she is confounded by her poverty and littleness:

> Lately my soul had been again in great travail. I cannot help constantly to consider how God deigned to call the spirit of Madonna House into being through so poor and weak an instrument as myself. You know that I consider this "religious, spiritual, lay family" a very special mandate of God to me as Foundress, and not only for myself but for others.   (SL #133, 1963)

> So I found out that a foundress first and foremost means a most thorough cleansing of one's soul: there are all kinds of trashy stuff in the endless and strange corridors, nooks, and corners of my heart, mind and soul.

> Being a foundress means also, I have discovered, being truly NOTHING! For, very slowly — tremendously slowly — as if drop by drop, God finally reveals the true essence of things. It is as if he were right there, sitting at my table and saying very simply: "Catherine, now you have to begin to understand that everything that has happened to you has been because of Me. Now you know that you are indeed NOTHING, for I AM EVERYTHING!

"You also have to begin to understand that this NOTHING is filled with Me, or is beginning to be filled. Remember how I said to you, "Without Me you can do nothing." (SLFF 1, 1970)

Insignificant

In one of the most beautiful of all Catherine's letters to us she gives her teaching on doing little things out of great love for God. We shall see more of it when we consider that particular line of the Mandate. Within this letter she presents her fundamental insights about the intuition of littleness. Again, her inspiration comes from a saying of St. Francis: "Lord, I throw my life at your feet and sing and sing that I give you such a small thing." When we consider what Christ has done for us, anything — our whole life, a thousand lives — are as nothing:

> For there before my eyes is a crucifix — living, breathing, full of wounds —saying to me: "I love you, I love you." When I measure myself against that crucifix, then my whole life is as nothing.

> So, to begin with, I consider *in toto* my whole life — from the day He called me to the day that I am speaking to you — A TINY LITTLE THING, in proportion to what He gave to me.

> To me, my life is as nothing to give to him. I wish that I had a thousand lives to give to him.

> Probably to you persecution would be a "big thing." But I can't visualize anything big. I am so small, so unworthy. I have only a life to throw at his feet, and it is so small! He gave me *His life*, and he is God!

Always consider everything you do as very small because what he gives you is so very big. Everything in
relation to God is small.   (SL #104, 1962)

Unimportant, Unpretentious

Pride has destroyed many a call from God. Who knows
the innumerable, authentic calls people have received from
God which have been corrupted and rendered fruitless by
pride. People forget that they were not chosen because of
their greatness, but because of God's love and mercy. After a
while we are tempted to think we were chosen because we
are great, forgetting that our humble acceptance of the call
is the only element that can truly make us great.

Like all authentic works of God, Madonna House was
born in obscurity, in the poor districts of Toronto, in
Harlem, in the small village of Combermere, Ontario. The
call of God does not make us small: Everyone *is* small. The
call simply challenges us to accept our smallness in relation
to the immensity of the mission and the election. Catherine
was always concerned that we remain small in this sense of
an awareness of our unimportance. Everything comes from
God, so we should never "pretend" it is due to our own
greatness and virtues. She also had a fear of "popularity."

I always visualized something that I thought would
please Christ. In his life, he hobnobbed with poor, non-
important people. He healed and he served, predomin-
antly, unimportant people, I mean unimportant in the
world's eyes. So I always thought that Madonna House
would be a small place: Christ serving people.

I always thought of Madonna House as small. It was
humble, small, in the sense of being unimportant.
Perhaps I am stupid, but something in me is afraid. The

very popularity of Madonna House is its undoing. And I have a feeling that the devil rejoices in its popularity, because that is what is going to bring it down, fast and furious. Let each staff worker have a heart, wounded by the Lord, for the Lord. A poor heart, a humble heart, unpretentious, simple, a "no big-shot" deal.

(MHWII, #29)

Let us be content to be misunderstood. Let us be content to be maligned, to be "made little of." For aren't we small, if not in numbers (though we are that yet) then in importance? And let us not worry about it. For the Lord was small in Bethlehem, and those who are small in him will someday be BIG before his face — but not now. Yes, let us be small, humble, poor . . . ready to live with what we have . . . making our home in Bethlehem and Nazareth, now and forever.   (SL #34, 1958)

We live in an age of "religious personalities" where the media "blows up" people out of all proportion to who they really are. Jesus lived most of his life in obscurity; and even during his public life he often avoided crowds, not out of danger to his humility(!) but as an example to us. Popularity creates an image in people's minds. The person chosen by God must constantly remember who he or she *really is* — *the least and littlest of all God's people.*

Five Smooth Stones — And God

Catherine has another concept of littleness: God doesn't need much to accomplish his work! Jesus only had five loaves and two fish that day, but there were five loaves, two fish — and God! In Catherine's mind the important thing is to be ready and perfectly docile in God's hands for whatever he wants. She often uses the image of David slaying Goliath with only five smooth stones:

In the line of apostles we are the smallest, the littlest . . .
and there is his Son again, with the sling of his grace,
bending down into the brook of life and getting little
pebbles . . . you and me . . . to place in his sling. But it is up
to God to shoot. The little pebbles must just be there. Here
is the hand of the Lord, and here are the little pebbles.
They must be shiny, worked over by the water, ready and
still . . . still on the palm of God's hand for him to pick up
and put into his divine sling, to shoot wherever he wants
to. That's all. But, oh, what goes into those stones!
Chastity, poverty, obedience, humility, simplicity, death
to self, love. The little pebbles lie there in the palm of
God's hand, content to rest there.   (R, Nov., 1974)

Small Is Beautiful

Catherine applies "small is beautiful" to the future form
of the Madonna House Apostolate. She has never seen us as
growing into some super organization which then accomplishes things "on a grand scale." Her vision is always one of
smallness, humbleness, person-to-person activity:

Small is beautiful, You (Lord) want the staff to divide
in some sort of a way which is not quite clear to me . . . but
you will make it clear. For those who have gone through
the poustinia, and understood a little of sobornost, You
want them to become stranniki, that is, pilgrims. That
means that every staff worker will become a pilgrim, factu-
ally going where they are needed, or in perfect stillness,
attending to the needs of Madonna House.

(SLFF #96, 1978)

She quotes, in this letter, with approval, a few thoughts
from Karl Rahner:

The Church will be again a little flock of those sharing the same faith, the same hope, the same love. It will not pride itself on this, it will not think itself superior to earlier ages of the Church, but will obediently and thankfully accept its own age as is apportioned to it by the Lord and his Spirit. (*The Christian of the Future*).

Entering Hearts

In order to enter the Cave in Bethlehem you have to become small, like a child. As the vision of the Mandate unfolds you will see that we are on a journey into the human heart in order to reveal the love of the Heart of Christ. To enter the human heart, one must be very small:

> What am I saying? I'm trying to say that we must plunge into the dark night of faith. That while we cry out for the depths, our very crying becomes a stout cord, a sort of ladder, that brings men out of the pit of despair into the light of his Face. I'm trying to say that God is using us as he used the uncouth, unlearned apostles and disciples, for whom he thanked God, His Father, saying, "I thank thee, Father, Lord of heaven and earth, that you have hidden these things from the wise and learned and revealed them to mere children!"
>
> I'm trying to say that we must have one desire: to be those little ones, to allow ourselves to be used by him as he wished, no matter what the cost to us. For he brought us together . . . to do just that. The wise are confused. The wise are seeking their identity. The wise are worshipping a thousand idols. And we are being asked by the Lord to go into their hearts so as to bring them to him.
>
> But who of us dare venture into the caverns of men's hearts unless we be children? A child ventures anywhere. So I finish my letter, my dearly beloved in Christ, by

imploring him to truly GIVE US THE HEART OF A CHILD, AND
WITH IT THE AWESOME COURAGE TO INCARNATE IT.

Yes, let us become children, "for a little child shall lead
them." The theme for Madonna House, 1969, should be
this: OUR IDENTIFICATION WITH THE CHRIST CHILD. We
can give him our poverty, our helplessness — all that we
are (but maybe we shouldn't be). But this Christ Child is so
immense that, with just a glance, he will take away all the
dross from us if we let him. He will make us like unto
himself: A CHILD.

Now I know the poverty I bring you: IT IS THE POVERTY
OF THE CHILD IN BETHLEHEM.   (SL #259, 1968)

Littleness

Beloved, you know well my foolish heart. You have
beheld its foolishness so long you will not mind beholding
it again in all its littleness and fears, bewilderments and
tiny pains.

Beloved, it is like this. I am so truly small and worth
nothing at all, except in you.

My smallness is alright. It fits your hand well and you
know that you possess it so utterly as to absorb it fully. But
you love to let me go into a cloud where knowledge does
not dwell, and where all things are still and wrapped in
love and you.   (JI, I)

CHAPTER EIGHT

Simplicity

* * *

... Simple ... Poor ...

The words "little, simple, poor, childlike" swirl around in Catherine's mind like waters in a whirlpool, rushing to the center. The center of what? Being: What is it to *be*? As we continue with the next two words of the second line, you will see Catherine struggling to penetrate the essence of the being of the *child* before God. But hers is not an intellectual struggle for definitions, Catherine's thought develops, is forged, out of her desire to live the Gospel concretely. Her struggle to understand simplicity, for example, arises from her desire to identify with the poor:

> I went into the slums ... Obviously, I had to be simple, meaning not only simple in the scriptural sense of the word, but simple and direct; a person who faces the essence of things ... You see, I equated the word "simple" with a true identification with the poor ... Simple, to me, meant facing, without any rationalization, the type of life that I would have to undertake, and all its effects, results. I had to lay these out in utter simplicity, face them, and say a fiat to them.

Who can be simple? Who can always be little? A child. I had to be childlike in order to be simple and in order to be always little.   (HMCB)

Her original instinct, then, about simplicity, was that, in order to identify with the poor, she had to simplify her very complicated life, "leaving behind not only money, goods, but my intellect as well." Simplicity is to go to the essence of things, and here it means to go to the essence of the life of the poor who live on the bare essentials of life. "Going to the essence of things" is Catherine's key idea about simplicity; she then proceeds to speak about this essence in a variety of ways.

You might say that something is simple when it is just what it is. For example, we do not say of a tree or flower, "Oh, what a simple tree!" or, "Oh, what a simple flower!" Trees and flowers *are what they are*, so we don't say they are simple. We apply the word to things or people that have the potential to become complicated, that is, untrue to their being. We may say of a room, "How simply decorated it is," implying that it could be awfully overdone. We also use the word "simple" of people who are free from artifice and duplicity: they just are who they are.

Here is where Christ is also our model. We do not say that Jesus was a simple Person but simply a person. Jesus is like the trees and the flowers — simply and exactly as the Father intended him to be. It is arriving at this essence of the Father's original design that we call simplicity. In Jesus, being and doing and acting and speaking are all one: his life flowed from his essence. We are not in touch with our essence, and so our actions and lives are complicated, not simple.

In an early Staff Letter Catherine briefly spelled out some of the meanings of the word "simple":

Simplicity. The moment we apply this word to our spiritual life we get an interesting picture of a person who is single-minded, whose mind goes to the essence of things without embellishment . . . sophistication, or complications. It conjures up a person who is innocent of guile, one who is truthful, direct.

Holy simplicity is this state of mind and soul, totally, single-mindedly, lifted up and occupied by God. The colloquial word for holy simplicity would be childlikeness. This brings us immediately to the Gospel — "Unless you become like little children" — single-minded, uncomplicated, without embellishment, plain, without mental, intellectual, spiritual superfluities, free from affectation, sincere, artless, unsophisticated, humble, trusting — "you shall not enter the kingdom of heaven."

This is a topic vitally important nowadays because man is so complex, filled with fears and inhibitions, fragmented, and needs to be recollected above all in the *simplicity that goes to the essence of things.*   (SL #174, 1965)

Simplicity, Nazareth, Ordinariness

In one of her important letters on simplicity Catherine reminds us that God is simplicity itself. She then goes on to consider God Incarnate among us, and says:

There is no denying that we cannot understand the mystery of his simplicity; at the same time, a thousand wounds of ours would be healed if humbly and simply we approached him and asked him to allow us to become as simple as he was in our daily, nitty-gritty, uneventful (in a manner of speaking) existence.

What is more simple than the life of a carpenter in the midst of a small village? The very simplicity of his occupation must have been very monotonous, very hard on his muscles, perhaps even tedious. For simplicity is like that. It accepts the nitty-gritty way of life, the sameness of it, the monotony of it. But once understood (this monotony) is shot through with great joy. Simplicity holds within itself a fantastic joy. The nitty-gritty, everyday sameness of our lives would become shot through with songs of joy if we embraced simplicity. Our lives would become very much like the life of the Holy Family. Yes, the more we grow in simplicity, the more joyous we would become.

(SL #66, 1961)

In several places Catherine explains simplicity in terms of ordinariness. The two themes are very closely allied in her thinking.

"Order" is the root word for "ordinariness." When our lives are perfectly ordered according to God's will, we will be simple. We have seen the importance of the mystery of Nazareth for Catherine. Another aspect of this mystery is that Nazareth reveals to us God's presence in the ordinary, and teaches us how to divinize the ordinary:

The acceptance of the ordinary, of the commonplace, of the obvious, which is radiant with the glory of God since the resurrection of the Lord Jesus (is) the key to this stupendous mystery that is man. We are men and women of glory and power, provided that we understand the obvious and the commonplace.   (WL)

Catherine called SL 124 "the beginning of My Last Will and Testament." Thus its contents are extremely important. In the closing lines she expresses how important a treasure is this mystery of the ordinary:

I leave you one of the most beautiful gifts that God has given to me. I didn't give it to you — GOD GAVE IT TO YOU:

God showed you how to live the nitty-gritty life of the Gospel. And we are different from any other community because we have done that. And I would like you to continue. Especially cherish so much, cherish it like a great gift of God, that he has taught you to be ordinary. The ordinariness of our days in Madonna House, the simplicity of it, the hospitality of it — THAT IS THE ESSENCE OF MADONNA HOUSE.

Don't break that, because then the Face of God will disappear from you, and in no time. It didn't take long for Friendship House to break, nor will it take you a long time to break, if you are unfaithful to that ordinariness, to that simplicity, to that living of the Gospel in the reality of life.

And in another important statement, the same idea:

Can you catch a soap bubble? Is it easy to catch a butterfly on the wing? No. Nor is it easy to catch the spirit of Madonna House. It is the spirit that matters, nothing else does. What is this butterfly on the wing? What is this soap bubble that doesn't allow itself to be caught, but bursts into little pieces in your hand?

Very simple: Madonna House was built on humility, simplicity, ordinariness . . . merging with the poor, reflecting the icon of the Christ of the poor . . .   (MHWII #23)

As always, this journey to the ordinary is painful because of the pride and complexity due to sin. But it is especially in the ordinary that we will meet the lonely Christ and be remade into his image and likeness:

What will your love bring to your Beloved? You will bring to him stew well made; 3 x 5 cards correctly filed over and over again; endless potatoes finely peeled; floors eternally scrubbed so as to allow his feet in your neighbor's to walk across it; machinery kept clean day in and day out. Men will not know you for who you are. They did not know him in Nazareth. They will not understand you.

All this will make you more like your Beloved. All these little things are the fingers of God the Father shaping you unto the loneliness of his Son. Shaping you unto his hiddenness. Shaping you unto his pain. In proportion as you *are* these things, another portion of God's field will be restored to him. Simple is our vocation, so utterly simple that words fail to describe it.   (SMHA)

And, as the cross is the direct route to all the virtues, so it is with simplicity:

You speak so easily of Her they call Simplicity, but do you know the way to Her? It too is simple, like Herself.

Two beams that make a cross are simple, homey things to make of trees that grow abundantly. Their nails so easily come by, so cheap, so simple. A hammer, an old, familiar tool that will do nicely!

Now, your hands and feet — simple parts of you! You will find Simplicity. The way will be quite simple, straight, and clear — when wood, nails, and you are one! Then she is yours!   (SL #66, 1961)

Simplicity And The Preaching Of The Gospel

There are three themes here: If one is simple one will
(1) preach the Gospel *with boldness* and without fear;
(2) the preaching will be *simple*; and
(3) the message will be passed on *without distortion.*

Boldness in preaching the truth:

Yes, simplicity walked with him through all his journey, for simplicity is fearless. True, he was God. He did the will of his Father. But then, he made us gods too, for he made us brothers and sisters of himself, and heirs of his Father. And because of his love for us he preached and taught us to love God back in a simple, childlike way, a way that would not be afraid to tell (preach) the truth; because if we accept his simplicity we will never imagine that *we* are doing it. We will know, know for sure, that it is *he who preaches in us.* Yes, we will know that, if our hearts are simple. (SL # 66, 1961)

Priests especially should imitate Christ's simple preaching style:

So you see what I mean by simplicity. I see a priest sitting in the midst of other people, not even on a platform or anything, but just sitting and talking, telling of the marvels of God, the way God would talk about them. Simplicity is the fruit of love. Only love can be simple. I remember when I was with my mother once in Jerusalem and we went outside the city. The place was filled with red poppies. My mother looked at me and said, "You know, it is so easy to visualize Christ sitting on the little stones here and perhaps brushing the poppies with his feet. People would come and listen to the beatitudes." I have often sat in the imaginary poppy field . . . and listened to Christ explain the Gospel. It is the simplicity, that authenticity, that something that comes from the heart and not from a book, that I would especially like the reverend clergy to give us. (MHWII, #16)

One must be simple in order to receive and pass on the Gospel *as it is*:

Our century is not simple. You and I, to become simple as he wants us to become, must undergo a kenosis, must stop rationalizing the Gospel away . . . To be simple is to accept the essence of the message and not try to twist it, to adapt it to our ideas. We don't want to be so complex that we make God into our image, instead of remaining the image of God. (She then uses the image of a plastic hose we received in donation as an image of simplicity.)

This is simplicity, to be a clear, plastic hose so that the clear, divine waters of Christ . . . can go through. How simple you have to be for that, how deep your kenosis. (COLM)

Simplicity As A Remedy For "Serious Virtue"

In *Not Without Parables* Catherine has a delightful story entitled "How Humility Grew Into Simplicity." Really, it could be about almost any virtue which has become too "serious" and thus lost the freshness and spontaneity of a child. "She (Humility) looked at herself, examining all her motives and intentions as was her custom. She found herself still lacking something she could not define. Could it be that *what she was* — Humility — kept her from playing with the Child?" She had been invited by this Child in Nazareth to play ball, but she could not:

The Child kept cocking her head to one side, surveying her thoroughly. Then, speaking quite distinctly, told her that she needed to grow. Her growth should be downward, into littleness. He sang a song to her:

Come on, get small. Come and play ball with me. And then you will grow very big, my dear Humility. Because you will meet Simplicity, and she will teach you how to be like me.

And then you will understand that it is not enough to know your nothingness, but that to grow and grow with me you have to be Simplicity.

And then you will be all filled with Charity. Come, play ball with me. I am Simplicity; and I will teach you how to be as simple as me!

Without childlike simplicity — the ability to play with God in self-forgetfulness — all the virtues remain in their "serious" adult stage!

The above are the main themes. Also scattered throughout her works is simplicity equated with:

(1) kenosis: when you are empty of self you will be simple;

(2) dependence: "Imagine Christ as a Baby totally dependent on human beings. So simplicity is dependency. As the Lord depended on his creatures, so we, his creatures, should depend on him";

(3) Christ-likeness: "Simplicity is Christ-likeness, to live according to Christ's lifestyle."

Simplicity As The Essence Of Madonna House

Although there are several mysteries and virtues which Catherine characterizes as the "essence" of Madonna House, she does not use this word lightly or indiscriminately. I think it is very significant that in some of her final statements (in MHWII) about the nature of Madonna House, simplicity is foremost in her mind:

I pray that all members of MH really begin to understand its simplicity. (1)

I said that MH was born out of simplicity. (3)

MH is founded on such simplicity that nobody can understand how deeply MH is founded upon Christ's simplicity. (5)

I repeat, like a parrot: simplicity, total, complete simplicity, an approach to the world that is like a child's approach, trusting ... (8)

Simplicity that should be the essence of Madonna House. (17)

I understood that Our Lord was drawing my attention to the great simplicity of Madonna House. (17)

What is the spirit of MH? Very simple. MH was built on humility, simplicity, ordinariness. It was humble, exceedingly simple, totally ordinary. (23)

And finally she equates simplicity with love:

I consider that Madonna House above all is simple. By simplicity I mean many things. Perhaps I should say that Madonna House is charitable, or should be, because simplicity and charity are very much alike; they have much in common. Perhaps simplicity is just the fruit of charity, because simplicity is certainly not ambitious for any great gifts of any kind. Simplicity is also truthfulness and directness and, like love, is always patient and kind and is never jealous. Simplicity implies openness and an attitude to life that is Christlike. Through simplicity the soul enters into Christ's life and can give it to others. (16)

For Catherine, simplicity is one of the great keys to the mystery of Nazareth. As a state of being it will cost a great deal. T.S. Eliot said that "Christianity is a condition of complete simplicity, costing not less than everything." We have lost God as our center, so everything has become very complicated — the apostolate, human relationships, virtue —

everything. Simplicity is the key which unlocks the door to the essence of things. Although it is within our grasp, the journey to reach simplicity is immense.

The Way
by G.K. Chesterton

The way is all so very clear
That we may lose the way.
So very simple is the road
That we may stray from it.

We walk bewildered in the light
For something much too plain for sight
And something much too clear to say.

Go humbly; Humble are the skies.
And low and large and fierce the stars.
So very near the Manger lies,
That we may travel far.

... Poor ...

In Chapter Three we treated of the spiritual foundations of Catherine's thinking on poverty. I remarked that I would not be considering her teaching on *material* poverty since much of this would only apply to our own community, or to those called to a life of total dispossession.

"Poor" here in the second line, however, is of universal application, since it's another synonym for the *being* of the child before the face of the Father. And, because the poverty motif plays such an all-embracing part in her spirituality, "poor," in this line, would, I'm sure, be Catherine's first choice for what it means to *be*. In the beatitudes also, "poor in spirit" was the Lord's first choice in describing what openness to, and possession of, the kingdom really is. I treat here, then, briefly, some of her thoughts on *spiritual* poverty.

As always her vision begins with Christ. In a letter to her spiritual director in the early '40s she wrote:

> One thing I know: He did not "help" the poor as Friendship House helps them. He helped by *being* poor in a sort of different way from us. He did not *take upon himself* holy poverty. He *was* poor, without taking it on.   (FL)

The Lord, of course, was always exceedingly rich, even while among us. We called his state "poor" because he lacked all the things on which *we* so much depend and pride ourselves. What are some of the components, some of the elements, of true spiritual poverty? The first is humility, the recognition and acceptance of our complete dependence on God.

> The beginning is in acknowledging your own immense poverty. You have to realize, deeply, fully, that all you are, all you have, is from God. Once you make this truth of your poverty before God the very marrow of your thoughts, your life, your love, your body, in a word, your being, then you will become truly humble, then you shall walk in truth, walk in and with God.   (SL #148, 1963)

The Lord Jesus conveys this truth to us when he says he can only do what he sees the Father doing, can only say what the Father gives him to say; that his doctrine is not his own, etc. The Father *is* Jesus' life, whereas we, because of sin, have an illusion of a separate life of our own, independent of God.

> Poor in spirit means that we know how utterly dependent we are on God; in a word, to understand what it means to be a creature of God.   (R, Mar., 1966)

Another scriptural word for this attitude is *anawim*, the poor of Yahweh:

> Christ said, "Without me you can do nothing." The Christian must also remember he is an "anawim" — a poor man of Yahweh, the poor man of the Beatitudes. He will know he is a creature, totally dependent upon God. He will rejoice in this, because this is the essence of poverty.   (R, Aug., 1966)

> Anawim. The really poor people who *know* that they are poor. Poor because they are creatures. Poor because they know they are utterly dependent upon God. Oh, to become one! To become the poor people of God who "lean" on God, as the Scripture says. Who among us realizes that everything that is, everything we have, comes from God? Who among us rejoices in this poverty which is true riches because it is the knowledge of who he is and who God is?   (GWC, 104)

If the mandate from God is to "go to the poor," it is crucial for us to recognize our own inner poverty. Otherwise we will go as a "Lady Bountiful" to share with all those "poor people" our own abundant riches!

> *We* are the unknown land. Everyone is boarding a bus . . .to go and do something for the poor and the downtrodden. Am *I* not the poorest of all? Would I take a bus to discover my own need of God, my own utter poverty?

> What then is it that we have to bring to the poor? First, it seems the realization that we are the poorest of the poor. This is *the* question, and it concerns the very essence of poverty. Are we merely seeking to run away from facing our own poverty, and escape into the world of the poor?   (GWC, 100-101)

Thus, interior poverty is a stripping of the self which is a crucifixion, and which can only be accomplished through love:

> Poverty is a matter of a total change of our inner self. Such poverty can only be the child of love. For love alone can make man tear off all his masks, reveal himself as he is, and stand innerly naked before his fellow men!

> To say it is a painful process is to say nothing. It is the most excruciating thing . . . the hardest thing to do for a human being. It is to crucify oneself on the cross of Christ. And I think *that* is the goal of poverty. For only then will we truly draw all things to Christ as we are lifted up on that cross of poverty.   (R, Apr., 1963)

Scattered throughout her writings, Catherine equates this interior poverty with almost every virtue, so all-pervasive a concept is it for her. But one word approximates interior poverty more than all others — dispossession: "I am obsessed by something that is beyond poverty, or perhaps it is part of it, or perhaps it is the heart of it . . . I call it 'dispossession.'"   (SLFF #20, 1958)

In the following letter, written in 1972, are found some of her deepest expressions of interior poverty:

> A desire to possess a total emptiness of heart and mind, an emptiness in which a naked child could be born, big enough to contain a naked man on a cross.

> Does it sink deeply into your heart, mind, and soul that dispossession is *freedom*? If you dispossess yourself for Christ's sake, for God's sake, for love's sake, you are as free as the air.

> The dispossessed for Christ's sake are meek and therefore peacemakers. They are the gentle ones who use their

poverty, their dispossession, to wipe the tears of others. They are the humble ones, because they know that the greater is their dispossession, the deeper they are in the truth of God, and therefore totally humble.

One of the most consistent themes of Catherine about poverty throughout her whole life is that *obedience* is the crown, since it entails the dispossession of our free will:

> I began to understand that poverty would not grow unless obedience would walk with Her. For a soul must surrender not only its goods but itself. Obedience surrenders the will of a human being, truly his most precious possession, thus becoming the crown of poverty.
>
> (SL #94, 1962)

> He demands the death to self through poverty/obedience. He wants you to enter into the very heart of poverty . . . Obedience will make you truly *poor*. For through it, you will have surrendered that tremendous, magnificent, incredible gift of God — your free will — which is truly a free, loving gift from him.
>
> (SL #148, 1963)

> The naked, crucified One knows his own; but especially he cannot resist the ones who strip themselves inwardly naked for him, and immolate themselves on his own crucifix with him, for love of him and the souls for whom he died. Stripped in this fashion, dying to self, crucified on the cross of poverty and obedience, walking in humility (which is truth), you will be able to feel what the poor feel. You will heal, console, bring multitudes to God. You will be truly poor — in the full sense of that glorious word! — and hence, truly rich! (SL #148, 1963)

> Did it ever occur to you, dearly beloved, that to be totally dispossessed one must be totally obedient? Obedience is the crown of poverty. (SLFF #20, 1972)

As always, the deepening of each virtue is a way to console Christ in his ongoing passion:

> That hollowing out, which dispossession must make in our heart and soul to hold that naked child once born in a cave, to hold that naked man once crucified on a cross, is done by obedience.   (SLFF #20, 1972)

> Do we desire the Desired One? If so, do we wish to follow him and detach our hearts from all things that are not him, and be poor, not only in spirit but in reality? Are we going to share our immense surplus with the hungry ones of the world, the replicas of the Child?
>
> (R, Dec., 1967)

Every movement of the heart is intimately connected to Christ. When we are purified of our self-exalting attitudes, Christ comes to rest in us, a warm cave instead of his cold one, a companionable cross instead of his lonely one. And every person in material need with whom we share is a replica of the Child, a replica of the Man dispossessed on the Cross.

> Finally, this crib, this cross, created in our hearts by poverty, is not a negative space. It is charged with "joyousness" because the heart now adheres to God alone.
>
> (SL #40, 1959)

> The detachment and dispossession from all things is transformed into a "flaming love for all created things."   (SL #94, 1962)

> God himself is not detached from his creation. He loves everything passionately — but purely. This pure, passionate, joyous love for everything is the final goal of interior poverty, "a love that sings his glory alone."
>
> (SL #94, 1962)

Just as the goal of kenosis is plerosis, the fullness of the Christ-life in us, so the goal of poverty is a "flaming love" for all of creation, but a love now totally rooted in God.

The Spirit Of The Madonna House Apostolate

by

CATHERINE DOHERTY

* * *

The spirit of Madonna House is one of ardent zeal for the glory of God, the salvation of souls, and the restoration of all things to Christ through Mary. You have come here by inspiration of the Holy Spirit to dedicate your life in this very humble apostolate, hidden like the Holy Family of Nazareth — unknown, unsung, utterly indistinguishable, outwardly, from the rank and file of everyday humanity — except for a cross.

The second aim of this Apostolate is to restore man and his institutions to Jesus Christ through Mary in the lay apostolate by means of work in any phase of Christian reconstruction.

This is the work that you do. But the way that you are going to do it depends on who you are. What you do matters — but not much! Who you are matters tremendously.

The world is restored to Christ by being a servant: "Zeal for my Father's house consumes me. I cannot rest." This is you — unable to rest because you love. "I shall arise and go and find my beloved, for I cannot rest until my heart rests in him." Ours are the words, "I sleep but my heart watches." We are passionately, utterly, completely, in love with God, or should be, as we progress along this road of our Apostolate. We breathe, we live, we eat, we sleep, only for one reason: To serve him whom our hearts love, and to extend his kingdom.

You have heard the plan of God outlined for you well enough. The miracle of that plan is that God invites you and me to participate in it. What is that plan? Behold, the Crucifixion! A simple cross, and on it a Man who thirsts — *sitio*! Does he thirst for water? For wine? Maybe. But he thirsts above all for souls. The best gift of a lay apostle of Madonna House is simply the gift of his or her life. "I give you my life, Lord, because the zeal of your house consumes me. I desire to bring you souls to assuage your thirst."

That is our vocation; that is the spirit of the Apostolate; that is what will make it work. The moment that spirit is lost, the Apostolate is dead, even if it covers the earth. It matters not if we are many in number, if our shelves groan under the weight of books, if we have an army of nurses rendering services to the sick, if we are feeding the poor. Unless our hearts are filled with the charity of Christ, and we burn with the zeal of this charity, we are like sounding brass and tinkling cymbals. Without love, nothing that we do will matter. No restoration will follow. Our activities will only be extensions of things Communists and pagans do. The difference between us and them is motivation. We do these things because we cannot help doing them, because, like a people on fire, we must serve; otherwise our love for God will simply tear us apart! Love must serve!

Love is not an abstract thing. Love is not something that you can classify, weigh, organize. Love is a fire; it must spend itself in service. Service is the dry wood for love, that which turns it into a bonfire that reaches into eternity and burns even there! What you and I are called to be in the utter Stygian darkness of this world are flames. A lamp for my neighbor's feet. A place where he can warm himself. A place where he can see the face of God. How can people see in the dark?

It is to be, to love, to burn, that we have come together! And who brought us? The Fire of Love! the Holy Spirit! We are little flames, coming together, each growing, uniting in various patterns according to the call of God as expressed by the bishop. We are loving, burning, offering ourselves up in the holocaust! "I wish to burn, Lord, consume me. Take no notice of my weaknesses or difficulties. Shape me into your image and likeness."

Then we turn our faces to God the Father, the Immense Sculptor. Once we were clay, dust. Out of that clay he fashioned us. Blowing with his breath he made us come alive. Now, turning our faces to God the Father, we say in all simplicity: "Once more clay comes to you, but now clay with a free will. So, of my own free will, I come. Shape me into the likeness of your Son. I know that, before the face of the resurrected Christ can be shaped in my soul by your holy hands, I have to be shaped into the likeness of the Man of Sorrows. Shape me. For that is the purpose of my life, that is the desire of my soul — to be where my Beloved is. Here I am, Lord. Shape me!

And God the Father will bend towards me and you, and, in our poor human faces, shape the likeness of the Christ of Gethsemane, the Christ of Pilate, the Christ of Sorrows, the Christ who was persecuted, spit upon, flagellated, crowned with thorns, crucified. And then, someday, God the Father will come and say: "Now, arise, for I desire to shape you in the likeness of my Son in glory." That's our vocation. That's the spirit of it — an utter surrender that knows no bounds. What is death to me but entrance into life?

Do I fear man? What can he do to me? I walk in the shadow of God. Is anything impossible to me? To me, yes, but not to me and him. I cannot take a breath without him. But with him I move in utter faith towards the impossible.

Is it cold where I am going? My Lord is cold. If I go there, he will warm me. The wastes of the arctic hold no fear for me. Am I going to live in the broiling sun, and shall the heat of the day consume me? What does it matter? The fire of my soul is hotter than any sun! It is cool in the Sahara desert compared to what happens inside of me!

I burn with a fire that will never be quenched until it becomes one with the Fire, the Movement, that is the Most Holy Trinity! Nothing matters except the Lord of Hosts and his will.

The members of Madonna House should hear constantly these words: "I have come to do the will of the Father." And also these words of Scripture: "He was obedient unto death." Thus burning with love I am a holocaust, offered with a zeal that consumes me for the glory of my Father's house. How else can I surrender unless I hear these words, "I have come to do the will of my Father"?

With joy I say, "Lord, O Lord, I have come to do thy will. O Christ, I will do the will of thy Father also. For thy will and the Father's will are one." And so, in every moment of my day, in every step that I take, I see the will of God. The duty of the moment speaks to me in the accents of a Lover.

I am not doing the duty of the moment because the person in authority tells me to do it. I am doing it because my Lord spoke. Across the centuries I hear with the ears of my soul the voice of him whom my heart loves. And I arise, and I hasten to do the will of my Beloved.

This is the only way that I shall restore the world. The restoration of the world, which is the aim of our Apostolate, must come from within me, and from within each one of you. The key is this intangible reality — which is as strong as death, as strong as everlasting life — which is called love. Nothing can destroy it, unless we destroy it ourselves. It is the only motive, the only reason, for being here. Everything is senseless unless you are here for loving — utterly, passionately, completely. The very word "love" implies sacrifice and surrender.

"He was obedient unto death." Crosses are not fashionable in the 20th century. The Iron Curtain has not yet enclosed what we call the "Free Nations." The shadow of the Curtain has not yet fallen over you — but it might. That will be another kind of cross.

But the cross of Christ always casts its shadow over all of us. It is a simple death he calls us to, but, oh, how profound, how strange, how mysterious! It is a death which in itself carries the very seeds of life. It is a simple, profound, complete death to self which opens all doors. When the "I" has completely surrendered, then the hallways of the Kingdom of Heaven have opened upon the earth. Greater love has no man than to die for his fellow man. Our vocation is to die that we may live and give life to others. To the extent that I die, to that extent my neighbor lives, to that extent I bring the light of Christ.

I spoke of zeal and of fire and of light. But all fire and all light must have a container of some sort — a fireplace, a stove, a lamp — in which to burn. Death to self is that container. Death to self is the immense torch that we can lift on high to dispel the darkness. For what are we fighting against? We are fighting not only against the world, the flesh, and the devil, but against powers and principalities. And these can only be exorcised by love in the name of the Father and of the Son and of the Holy Spirit. Love is the mother of all virtues. Love is the fire that alone can push back the darkness of those powers and principalities.

These powers thrive in darkness; evil lurks in darkness; darkness covers up so many sins. It is so easy to doubt, to sow discord, to plant anger against each other in the darkness. What will dispel darkness? One thing: love.

Like a poisonous flower hatred flourishes in damp and dark places — in dead marshes, lakes, or rivers. From thence hate emanates its deadly, stiflingly sweet, putrid perfume. Who shall venture into the kingdom of death and hatred — real death, death to the soul? Only he who dies to self because he loves; only he who is obedient to the will of God; only he who is a lamp, a light, a torch, a bonfire, unafraid to walk alone into the darkness and conquer hatred. There is only one thing that conquers hatred: love! And nothing else except love ever will.

But how can I love if there is one millionth of an ounce of self in me? Love is a Person. Love is God. Where love is, God is. And our vocation is to make room for God in ourselves . . . if I may say so, to clothe God with our flesh, to once again give him hands and lips and eyes and a voice. But to do that we must die to self. God is immense. He needs much room — our whole being! No one crevice must be left to ourselves. Otherwise we maim Christ if we refuse him access to any part of us. And where is the lover who keeps back anything from the beloved? Such a person is not a true lover.

And so that is our vocation — to burn, to die, to become a flame, so as to make room for Christ to grow in us. Once the feet of Christ, through our feet, touch again this earth of ours, the earth will grow and be restored. Dedication is seen in pain. There is a radiance emanating from that pain which disperses the shadows in another's face. That is the essence of our vocation — to burn with love, to be a light, to be a fire. And, as you who live in this wooded environment know only too well, you cannot start a fire with green wood. No more will the fire of the love of God take hold in a soul that is not utterly dedicated to him.

You have no past, no future. You have no mother, no father. You have no wife, no husband. You have no children, no relatives. You are alone, facing your Lover, God. No one and nothing is between you and God.

You live between two Masses. You exist in the present moment. You do the will of him who sent you, for you are an apostle, and the word "apostle" means "one who is sent." Who sent you? Christ. Who sent Christ? God the Father. You are ready. You have nothing in your hands. How can you be an apostle with possessions? Your road is long; your road is dusty. You will be living in the alleyways and byways of the world. Yours is the stinking backyard. Yours are the places nobody wants to go to. Can you take any possessions there? Yours are the immense stretches of desert that exist in men's souls. You will have to cross the seas of despair and doubt in their hearts. Can you take any baggage on this strange journey? No! And so, to your obedience and love is added poverty.

You go forth as an apostle should. Take no shoes, no gold or silver. Then, once more you too will hear the words of Christ at the end of the journey, "Have you wanted anything?" Our vocation is simple, so utterly simple, that words fail to describe it. It is intangible, and yet very concrete. To burn. To do the will of God in the humble duty of every moment. To die to self through obedience, poverty, love. Through chastity also: to have no one who belongs to you, and you belonging to no one, except God. To live in the present moment. To be ready to be crucified (in the mystical sense) on the cross of the will of God. To be ready to be crucified by men. You will be. You will be crucified with their words, not yet realizing that words spoken by men are like chaff in the wind. They will be words of disapproval, of doubt, of ridicule. You will also be crucified by gestures (the shrugging of shoulders, for example). You will be crucified by others' disbelief in your way of life.

And I want you to understand your crucifixion. We are not worthy to be crucified high up on a hill. St. Peter even was crucified head downwards; and St. Andrew was crucified on a cross shaped differently from that of the Lord's. They were glad because of these differences. They felt they were unworthy to be crucified as Christ, who was God.

Our cross will be very small. It will probably be in the market place where we have our dwelling. The byways, the deserts, the alleyways, the stinking backyards — this is the market place, figuratively speaking. Our cross will be small, as tall as you or I, each according to his size.

And what will happen? A merchant will pass by, stop, poke his fat fingers into your mouth and into your eyes, into your chest and into your side, and say, "Humph, not much!" and pass by.

A lawyer will come around and say, "It's illegal to be crucified these days in the public market place. Humph! Wonder what they're made of?"

A doctor will pass by and say, "This is unhygienic; it shouldn't be allowed," and poke you some more. A woman, bent on everybody's business but God's, will stand there and say, "Humph," and go on to express her opinion of you to everyone in no uncertain terms. Priests will pass by and say, "How foolish." Nuns will come and say, "Neither fish nor fowl. Just look at them!"

Then somebody will come and throw mud (we don't deserve stones yet) and say, "Oh, pelt them also with rotten eggs." And somebody else will say, "Throw in a rotten to-matoe for good measure." And there, crucified by the will of God for your sanctification, you will stand, crowned with an invisible kingly cape, with rotten eggs and tomatoes for your crown of thorns.

Your daily life seemingly will be very dull. You have only one moment to live at a time. One day at a time between two Masses. You have no past. Your yesterdays are gone. You have no future. Your tomorrows belong to him. You have only today.

I have only this moment to do the will of the Father. Only this moment to be obedient unto death. Only this moment to burn with a fire that knows neither beginning nor end. Only this moment to spill myself out in service to my neighbor. For I must prove to my Beloved that I love him. Words are not enough! Words die before the Word. I can only prove my love for him by loving my neighbor, for my neighbor is He Himself.

What will your love bring to your Beloved? Are you going to bring beautiful vestments that you have sewn through the night with the finest of gold and silver threads? Will you bring him a crown of gold, or a scepter that you've spent half your lifetime carving out of priceless ivory? Are you going to bring Him poetic verses that will move multitudes, or music that will enchant the world? Are you going to bring Him books that will make Him better known? No! You will bring Him stew well made; endless potatoes finely peeled; 3 x 5 cards correctly filed over and over again; floors eternally scrubbed so as to allow His feet in your neighbor to walk across; machinery kept clean and oiled, day in and day out; garbage removed; endless trips through snowy wastes in the Yukon, or through the rough roads in Combermere, to bring someone to the hospital.

Years of this! You will bring such humble gifts that people seeing you carrying your offering to the sacrifice will shrug their shoulders and turn away their faces and say, "I thank you, Lord, that I am not like these."

They will not know you for who you are. They did not understand Christ in Nazareth for who he was. They will not understand; it will be hard for you to be misunderstood; it was hard for the God-Man to be misunderstood. But you will rejoice with a great joy, for all this will make you more like your Beloved.

All these little things are the fingers of God the Father, conforming you unto the loneliness of His Son, conforming you unto the misunderstanding that His Son suffered, conforming you unto Christ's hiddenness, unto his pain.

Slowly, the fingers of God's Will, and the fingers of time, will become one. You will be shaped and shaped, not knowing even that you were shaped. You will enter into a great darkness, a great aridity, a great temptation. But oh, rejoice! For this is the desert where Christ spent 40 days fasting! This is his hunger you are experiencing. This is the Lover paying court to your soul, hiding himself, as lovers are wont to do, so that you, whom he loves, might arise and go in search of him. The hide-and-seek of love, the eternal playfulness, is now lifted to a supernatural plane.

Be at peace! This darkness, this aridity, this desert, are joyful. They are the beginning of wisdom, for your Beloved is the very Wisdom of God. He teaches you His Wisdom, now in the loneliness and silence of the desert, now in the quiet and darkness of the night of love. There are two nights in this world: the night of hate and the night of love. This is the night of love.

All this is the spirit of our Apostolate. This is the warp and woof of the dedication that I am talking about. Without this spirit your own restoration is but chaff in the wind. Words are inadequate to explain this dedication rooted in love. Who can explain intangibles?

And so you shall go through life for many years as a sort of freak! But if you do, there will come a day when people will know you for who you are. And because you laid down your life in this death day after day, minute by minute; because you died to self in the duty of the moment; because with your unalterable will you were united with the will of God; because you laid down your life for your fellow man, unobtrusively, in a hidden way, without any trumpets sounding, without any acclaim — because of all this the world will have another portion of God's field restored to

Him. To the extent you do these things, to that extent the world will be restored, to that extent you shall become mighty against the darkness.

On that cross God will give you the strength to be a light, not only to your neighbor's feet, but a light that blinds the devil, and the powers and principalities. Then, in the name of the Trinity, you shall go forth into the dark and dank places, diving without fear into the still waters that run so deep, in order to rescue a soul. Then you will be ready. You will be ready because there will be no self in you. You have loved, and you have made room for God. What can you be afraid of when you are able to say, "I live now, not I, but Christ liveth in me"?

This is the goal of the Apostolate, to love as God wants us to live so as to be fearless. For the battle in which we are engaged demands courage. Perfect love alone casts out fear. Nothing else can cast it out. So let us learn to love perfectly.

Love is a Person, Love is God. We possess God in proportion as we love. And then, because God is never outdone in generosity, we possess Him because He wishes to be possessed. He comes to us in the deserts and the dark nights, and they are no more. Then we know the Light because we have brought the Light.

It is a strange vocation that you are entering — luminous, full of light. The only thing that can make it dark is yourself — if you do your own will and not the will of God the Father and the Son, which are identical.

In everyday life, as you trudge through this vale of tears, you will constantly be looking for the Promised Land. But you love God so much that you are not concerned when He will call you home. A time will come when you will wish to die simply because living is so difficult. But even then you will say, "O.K." You will be more interested in His will than in going to heaven, for it may not be His will that you be in heaven now.

And so, in everyday life, what do we expect of you, or rather, what does God expect of you? A great simplicity, an absolute naturalness, a humility as ordinary as the air. For who are we? In the line of apostles we are the smallest, the littlest. We are lay people — consecrated, dedicated — but lay people. We are very small. Remember what I always say. David looked at Goliath and saw a brook. In the brook he saw little pebbles; and he had a childish sling-shot. He bent down and picked up those pebbles, put them in his sling, and slew the mighty Goliath.

The Lord does likewise with us. David is a prefiguration of Christ. The Lord looked at the world and saw the goliaths of darkness waxing strong and fat, plucking away from Him the souls for which His Son died. Christ His Son, with the sling of His grace, bends down into the brook of life. He picks up little pebbles, you and me, to fix into His sling. What must we do as lay apostles? The little pebbles must just "be there." It is up to God to shoot.

Here is the hand of the Lord, and here are the pebbles. They were worked over by the water. They are shiny and ready. They lie still on the palm of God's hand. It is for Him to pick them up, put them into His divine sling, and shoot wherever He desires. That's all!

But oh! what goes into those tiny pebbles! Chastity, poverty, obedience, humility, simplicity, naturalness, death to self, and love. The pebbles lie still in the palm of God's hand, content just to rest there.

How are you going to achieve all this? What's the program? It's superhuman; let's call it supernatural. The only way you can acquire the strength to lie still in the palm of God's hand, to die to self in the unglamorous and monotonous duty of the moment, is prayer. A trip to Nigeria, to Brazil, to Europe, will be glamorous for a month or two. But then, the backyards of Paris, the alleyways of Ceylon, the rural roads of Nigeria, the broiling sun here, the humid climate there, this monotony will take hold of you again.

There will be new faces, but with the same old problems. There will always be the same treadmill — the feeding of souls, the feeding of bodies, the clothing of the naked, the nursing of tired minds and bodies. It will always be the same story repeated ad nauseam and ad infinitum. To someone experiencing these things for the first time they will be new and exciting. But for you it will be an old gramophone record. What is going to make this gramophone record exciting and pulsating with life?

The Lord! The vocation to love will give you the courage, the all-consuming zeal, to listen again and again, to clothe the naked again and again, to nurse the sick again and again, to feed the hungry again and again — and all with the zest of a young person on his or her first date!

As the years go by you shall see the Face of your Beloved. Slowly, the thousand and one faces that told you their story, that asked for help, will take on the shape of one Face. Then, slowly, very slowly, you will touch your Beloved before you die. This is the only reward of your vocation, the reward of your faith. We can touch Christ in the Eucharist with our lips, we can touch Christ in the priest. But always — at any time and in any place — we can embrace our Beloved, in the real sense of the word, by embracing our neighbor.

In the dark splendor of the grayness of every day, your days will be like a rosary without mysteries, like one long string without interruption. And yet, the whole rosary is a mystery of love, the love of a soul in search of God. Drop by drop, the beads of your days will drop into time. Gray days, gray beads — they are really the splendor or the incomprehensible fire that renews the face of the earth, restores the sick to health, raises the dead to life, helps souls come back to God.

Such is your vocation. It is strangely hidden, like a rich pearl in the gray, flabby body of an oyster. It is so simple. But you have to pray to be able to endure the monotony of those gray days, to be able to hear your days falling into time. You must believe that they are being gathered somewhere in eternity by God. You have to pray, pray without ceasing.

At first you are taught to pray in time. Pray the Mass of course, always. The Mass is the center, the heart, the essence of our faith. It is the fire into which you must plunge to become a flame. It is your rendez-vous with God. It is the only place where you and Christ become one in the reality of faith and life. The Mass is the food that will keep you on the treadmill of those gray days, chained without chains to the duty of the moment, for love is not a chain.

You are going to pray the prayer of meditation, through which your feet will run and explore the life of Him whom your heart loves, the mind of Him whose will you desire to accomplish with such a flaming desire, because you are all His.

You are going to learn how to pray vocally, and with your body.

All these things you will learn. They will give you courage; that is why you are learning them. They will give you strength to lie still on the palm of God's hand. You will learn how to pray always, to understand the mystery of the words "ora et labora" — prayer is work and work is prayer. Then some day you will reach that simple prayer of the presence of God where today in faith you will possess Him whom tomorrow you shall possess in the reality of eternal life. It will come.

Strange things will happen to you then. They will be new/old, shining gray things which are part of your holy vocation. They will be signs of contradiction, signs of the Lord of Hosts.

You shall see and understand that, far from being gray, your days are resplendent with glory if lived by dying to self, burning with zeal and love, desiring only one thing — the will of God. Splendor will walk with you, a splendor that you will scarcely understand.

Moses went up a mountain and there God spoke to him. Moses came down, and his face shone so much that the people were afraid. He had heard the voice of God. But you, my friends, when you are a holocaust of love, when you are surrendered as your holy vocation calls you to be, you won't merely hear the voice of God. You will belong to God! You are one with Him. You do not live but Christ lives in you! You will not be able to see how much your soul shines, but this shining is the essence of the restoration of the world to Christ. This is the splendor which illuminates and spills over into works of love.

But I needn't speak to you about works. I must talk about the Spirit. It's hard to find words to describe that spirit. It's so simple, yet so stupendously splendid that I falter. All similes that come to mind seem dead before I speak them.

This I tell you: you have seven years and nine months to think over your utter dedication; your final promises are for life. Woe to you if you wound this little Apostolate of the Lord by the breaking of charity! The only thing that can kill the Apostolate instantly is uncharitableness! Far from pushing the darkness out, you will allow it to enter. Instead of adventuring from the kingdom of hate, you shall bring hate in.

Whoever is going to be Director General in the years to come, into whoever's faltering hands the spirit of this Apostolate will be placed, be watchful, day and night over only one thing: love. Never mind the discipline! Never mind anything! It will come. But I charge you, with all the power that I have, in the name of everything I stand for, I charge you: Watch day and night, with the watchfulness of a hawk, with the watchfulness of a mother over her children, with the watchfulness of a shepherd over his flock, watch for any breach of charity. Woe to him or her responsible for that breach of charity! They bring death to the very spirit of the Apostolate, remember that!

Our vocation is of God, simple and humble. The psalmist says that there is a rock, and in the rock there are little crevices where the birds can nestle. The rock, of course, is Christ. "Big people," like John the Baptist, lay on his breast. Little people, like us, nestle in the crevices of his hand, or perhaps of his neck. We are so small. He who loves can nestle anywhere in the arms of the Beloved. Our vocation is that of nestling. How nice it is to nestle in Christ! Much goes into this privilege of nestling. Give much, and you will receive much in return. You will receive God, who is never outdone in generosity.

If people ask you, "What is the Apostolate of Madonna House?" you answer simply, "It is an Apostolate to love.

Where love is, God is. We desire to be God in the midst of the world. We are dedicated to the restoration of the world — man and his institutions — to God. The only way we can restore them is by loving, by having God within ourselves, a living flame."

The rest will follow. That's all there is to it: love and death. This is life everlasting in Christ. That's everything.

I haven't spoken at length about Our Lady; a brief mention at the beginning. This is because, for me, it is so self-evident that he who seeks Christ without Mary seeks Him in vain. All the things I have spoken about to you presuppose Christ, the Way to the Father. He said, "I am the way." But the gate to the way is Mary. And we are *domus dominae*, the House of Our Lady. Should one need to mention the evident?

All the things I have spoken to you about will happen to you if you go to Jesus through Mary. She possesses the secret of prayer, the secret of wisdom, for she is the Mother of God. Who else can teach you to burn with the fire of love except the Mother of fair love? Who else can teach you to pray except the woman of prayer? Who else can teach you to go through the silence of deserts and nights, the silence of pain and sorrow, the solitude of joy and gladness, except the woman wrapped in silence? Who can span the bridge between the old and the new, the "dedicated you" and the "undedicated you"? Only Mary, the bridge between the Old Testament and the New, the Jewish girl who brought forth the Messiah, the Son of the Almighty.

Sometimes it is difficult to speak of the self-evident. Without Mary, how can one speak of God the Father, who was so well pleased with her that he made her the Mother of His Son? How can we speak of Christ (who was her Son begotten by the Holy Spirit) without speaking of Mary, the spouse of the Spirit? Our Lady of the Trinity, and Our Lady of Madonna House, are one and the same.

Such is the spirit of our Apostolate. Perhaps my silence about Mary was a tribute to the woman wrapped in silence. But I conclude by saying that all that we do in this Apostolate we do through Mary. All of us are consecrated to her as her slaves. That's why we are free. And that is why we can dedicate ourselves so utterly to her Son, because it is she who shows us the Way.

Lovingly yours in Mary,

CATHERINE

(*A talk given March 22, 1956 — SL #140*)

Key To Cited Works

* * *

So as not to get too complicated, I have devised a key to Catherine's writings. Many works quoted in this book have not been published. If and when they are published the references will be different. So there didn't seem any point in getting too specific (page numbers, for example). Except for the community of Madonna House, people will not have access to the original works. For her published works I will most of the time give the page reference, though sometimes I am working from original manuscripts. Thus, in most cases, I will simply quote the work. I hope this will be sufficient and add to the simplicity of the whole. I list here also works I haven't cited in the book, to give the reader an overall view of her writings.

The alphabetical order is according to the *key* and not the work itself.

AF - *Apostolic Farming*. Private printing.

CI - "The Church and I." Unpublished, undated talk.

COLM - "Comments On The Little Mandate." Unpublished talk, 1967.

DB - *Dear Bishop* (New York: Sheed and Ward, 1947).

DF - *Dear Father* (New York: Alba House, 1978).

DLR - *Doubts, Loneliness, Rejection* (New York: Alba House, 1981).

DSem - *Dear Seminarian* (Milwaukee: Bruce Publishing Company, 1950).

DSis - *Dear Sister* (Milwaukee: Bruce Publishing Company, 1953).

FH - *Friendship House* (New York: Sheed and Ward, 1946).

FL - Furfey Letters. Catherine's correspondence with her spiritual director, Fr. Paul Furfey, when she was in Harlem.

FML - *Fragments of My Life* (Notre Dame, IN: Ave Maria Press, 1979). Catherine's autobiography.

GPW - *The Gospel Of A Poor Woman* (Denville, NJ: Dimension Books, 1981). Meditations on the Gospel of Matthew.

GWC - *The Gospel Without Compromise* (Notre Dame, IN: Ave Maria Press, 1976).

HA - *The History Of the Apostolate*. 3 Vols. Unpublished. Catherine's personal account of the history of her apostolate starting in Toronto, then continuing in Harlem and Combermere.

HMCB - "How The Little Mandate Came To Be." Unpublished talk, 1968.

ILI - *I Live On An Island* (Notre Dame, IN: Ave Maria Press, 1979).

JI, I & II - *Journey Inward.* This refers to two vols. of Catherine's poetry, privately published here at Madonna House. I refer to it either as JI, I or JI, II. Some of these poems have been published. See next ref., and *Lubov.*

JI - *Journey Inward* (New York: Alba House, 1984).

LDM - "Local Directors' Meetings." These are talks given at our yearly meetings here at Madonna House. Unpublished.

L - *Lubov* (Locust Valley, New York: Living Flame Press, 1985). Some of her poetry.

M - *Molchanie* (New York: Crossroad Publishing Co., 1982).

MHWII - *Madonna House, What Is It?* Unpublished manuscript, 1980.

MRY - *My Russian Yesterdays* (Milwaukee: Bruce Publishing Company, 1951).

NWP - *Not Without Parables* (Notre Dame, IN: Ave Maria Press, 1977).

OC - *Out Of The Crucible.* Some Ideas On Training For The Lay Apostolate. (New York: St. Paul Publications, 1961).

OLUM - *Our Lady's Unknown Mysteries* (Denville, NY: Dimension Books, 1979).

P - *Poustinia* (Notre Dame, IN: Ave Maria Press, 1975). Catherine's classic, now in over half a dozen languages.

Pov - *Poverty.* Unpublished manuscript. Catherine's final, comprehensive statement on this aspect of the Gospel. 1980.

PTW - *The People Of The Towel And The Water* (Denville, NJ: Dimension Books, 1978). Her best description of the Madonna House way of life.

R - *Restoration.* The monthly newspaper of the Madonna House community. (Only $2.00 a year!)

SC - *Stations Of The Cross.* A Meditation. Private printing, 1954.

SL - *Staff Letters.* Unpublished Letters of Catherine to her community.

SLFF - *Staff Letters From The Foundress.* A new series of the above, beginning in 1970.

SMHA - "The Spirit Of The Madonna House Apostolate." A talk given in 1956. See Appendix A.

SMS - *Soul Of My Soul.* Reflections From a Life of Prayer. (Notre Dame, IN: Ave Maria Press, 1985).

So - *Sobornost* (Notre Dame, IN: Ave Maria Press, 1977).

St - *Strannik* (Notre Dame, IN: Ave Maria Press, 1978).

T - *Tumbleweed.* (Milwaukee: Bruce Publishing Company, 1948). Life of Catherine by her husband, Eddie Doherty.

TOLM - "Thoughts on the Little Mandate." Unpublished talk at the Directors' meeting, 1969.

U - *Urodivoi*, Fools For God (New York: Crossroad Publishing Co., 1983).

WL - "Way of Life." The official Constitution of Madonna House written by Catherine, 1970-71.

WLIGI - *Where Love Is, God Is* (Milwaukee: Bruce Publishing Co., 1953).

Background Bibliography

* * *

Arseniev, Nicholas. *Russian Piety* (New York: St. Vladimir's Seminary Press, 1964).

Augustine, St. *Sermo de Ascensione Domini*, Mai 98, 1-2; PLS 2, 494-495.

Evdokimov, Paul. *Le Christ dans La Pensee Russe.*

Fedotov, George P. *The Russian Religious Mind* (2 Vols.) (Woodside, New York: Nordland Publishing International, Inc., 1976).

Marrevee. *The Ascension in the Works of St. Augustine.*

Mersch, Emile. *The Theology of the Mystical Body.*

Rahner, Karl. *The Christian of the Future* (New York: Crossroad, 1976).

Thunberg. Lars. *Man and the Cosmos.*

Zernov, Nicolas. *The Russians and Their Church* (New York: St. Vladimir's Seminary Press, 1977).